# The Reference Library User:
# Problems and Solutions

Forthcoming topics in *The Reference Librarian* series:

# The Reference Library User: Problems and Solutions

Edited by
Bill Katz

School of Library & Information Science
State University of New York at Albany

The Haworth Press
New York • London

*The Reference Library User: Problems and Solutions* has also been published as *The Reference Librarian*, Number 31.

The Haworth Press, Inc. 10 Alice Street, Binghamton, NY 13904-1580
EUROSPAN/Haworth, 3 Henrietta Street, London WC2E 8LU England

**Library of Congress Cataloging-in-Publication Data**

The Reference library user : problems and solutions / edited by Bill Katz.
    p.   cm.
    Also published as The Reference librarian, no. 31.
    Includes bibliographical references.
    ISBN 1-56024-022-9
    1. Reference services (Libraries) 2. Libraries and readers. 3. Reader guidance. 4. Problem solving. I. Katz, William A., 1924– .
Z711.4.R42   1990
025.5′2 – dc20                                 90-45731
                                                                           CIP

# The Reference Library User:
# Problems and Solutions

## CONTENTS

# ABOUT THE EDITOR

**Bill Katz**, editor of *The Reference Librarian*, is internationally known as one of the leading specialists in reference work today. He is currently a professor at the School of Library and Information Science, State University of New York at Albany. In addition to the two-volume *Introduction to Reference Work*, he is the author of *Magazines for Libraries* and *Reference and On-line Services: A Handbook*. Past editor of *RQ*, the journal of the Reference and Adult Services Division of the American Library Association, Bill Katz currently edits a magazine column in *Library Journal*. He is also the editor of *The Acquisitions Librarian*.

# Introduction:
# The Individual and Library Service

Early in her study of what has gone wrong with bibliographic instruction, Sheila S. Intner asks the important question — who is the public. Well, to answer not in her words, but from experience, the public is similar to love, taxes and death. Everyone knows what they are, but who can adequately define them. We just have to go on faith that most of us do know what "public" means in the context of reference services, and it is with what Intner rightfully calls that "amorphous entity" that this issue is concerned.

Not quite. Again, Intner is perfectly correct when she says it is a "mistake to define public carelessly." The librarian is dealing with individuals, not definitions. And it is with these individuals the authors in this issue are involved. There are almost as many points of view as there are public, but if anything is common to all the contributions it is a respect for those who seek assistance at the reference desk.

There are many problems and few solutions, although all offer suggestions which will at least help the user and help the librarian on a day by day approach to questions and answers. Some of the work with the public may be thankless, but it is flecked with just enough appreciation, just enough difficulty to never make it dull. Come then, and meet the pleasures, and not a little of the grief of public service.

Sherlock Holmes, turning to Watson, dismissed his problem with a simple truth: "You know my methods. Apply them." Nothing serves as a better introduction to Rubin's views on the "angry public." It leads off the series because it is involved with a common situation too little considered in the literature. Everything from here, too, is up.

Special services, for example, are a great treat for a bewildered public and Low demonstrates what can be done when a library is dedicated to more than simply acquiring data and giving it out on demand. The California program is one which would make us all heroes in our time. Read on. As one should the careful research by Cannon into the failure of the academic library to draw all of the public into its folds. Relevancy is the key, at least for the students, and certainly for the often unforgotten potential user — academic staff other than faculty. Solutions are suggested, too, on how to make a nonuser into a part of the library public.

An echo of the Cannon piece is found in Boulanger's study of the publics in academic libraries. Of course it is more than an echo, it is a contribution based on the realities of service at one state supported library. The helpful hints are everywhere and lucky the public that has Ms. Boulanger behind the reference desk.

There are many publics, and Wong-Cross reminds us of the services which should be offered the blind and physically handicapped. More important he suggests how this may be facilitated through the publications of the Library of Congress. An extremely useful and major approach, this should be required reading (in the view of the editor) of all librarians serving (or not serving) this public. Weingand calls "the invisible client" another type of person with a disability — the learning block. She gives the reader a detailed account of what can be done to help, and this, too, is among the required reading items.

By way of a counterpoint to the primary arguments put forth, Buschman points out the role played by the information broker in today's information world. There are many obvious and perhaps not so obvious conflicts which he examines. "Our traditional anxiety about image, combined with the high status of information technology, has led us into some uncritical approaches . . ." Beyond that, Buschman offers a neat solution.

*Bill Katz*

# I. HELPING THE PATRON:
# A LOOK AT REFERENCE ENCOUNTERS

## Providing More Than Just an Answer

### Kathleen Low

**SUMMARY.** The State Information and Reference Center of the California State Library provides a number of special services for its patrons. These services include compilation and distribution of publications such as *Management Trends*, a selective annotated bibliography focusing on current trends in business and management, and *Special Topics*, an irregular series focusing on topics of current interest such as childcare, biotechnology and illiteracy. Other services include providing patrons with direct access to the University of California's online catalog, and indirect access to hundreds of commercial databases. As a service to our very busy patrons, library staff will also gather and send library materials to the offices of patrons who request the service.

Once upon a time there was a library whose magnanimous task was to shelter the written knowledge of civilization. So, all the writings and books were gathered from the people and randomly stacked on tables in a cavernous building so the knowledge would be available to all. Unfortunately few scholars could ever find the

Kathleen Low is Library Systems Specialist, California State Library, P.O. Box 942837, Sacramento, CA 94237-0001.

documents they sought, and the laymen usually gave up looking for the information they desired. Needless to say, the library met an early demise.

Gone are the days when libraries needed only to collect, house, organize, and provide access to its materials. And gone are the days when providing library assistance meant directing patrons to the proper subject area. For today's libraries are information "products" manufactured by library staff. They are developed, enhanced, packaged, and marketed to the public. As with any product, their longevity in the marketplace depends upon their quality, appeal, cost, usefulness, and necessity.

Provision of reference services is an important component of the information product. It must also maintain a high level of quality and appeal. To this end, the California State Library's State Information and Reference Center provides more than just an answer.

## INTRODUCTION TO THE CALIFORNIA STATE LIBRARY

The California State Library was first established in 1850 to provide legislative reference assistance to state government. At that time the library resided in an apse on the east side of the State Capitol building.[1] Today the library occupies space in five buildings and employs a staff of over one hundred and sixty, of which over fifty are professional librarians.

The library is divided into two bureaus — the Library Development Services Bureau and the State Library Services Bureau, with one administrative unit supporting the operations of the entire library. The Library Development Services Bureau administers federal and state library grant programs and provides consulting assistance to libraries. The State Library Services Bureau is responsible for providing direct library services to the state legislature, state government employees, and Northern Californians unable to read conventional print materials. The bureau also provides interlibrary loans and reference assistance to public libraries. This bureau contains six public service units.

## California Section

As one of the library's missions "to collect, preserve and disseminate information regarding the history of the state,"[2] the California Section has amassed materials on all aspects of life in California from before its statehood to the present. The collection contains a variety of materials ranging from sheet music and manuscripts to crate labels and carved wooden boxes. The collection is widely known for its materials on the Gold Rush period and the Mother Lode.

## The Sutro Library

Complementing the California Section's collection, the Sutro Library, a branch of the library located in San Francisco, features the rare book and genealogy collections of the late Adolph Sutro. Regarded as the finest genealogy collection in the Far West, patrons can access over 9000 family histories, indexes of passenger ship arrival lists for major Eastern ports prior to 1900, census data, city directories, and other resource materials. Special collections include Mexican history and literature from the conquest to 1900, Hebrew manuscripts and scrolls, papers of Sir Joseph Banks, President of the Royal Society, and histories of printing and book illustration.

## Government Publications Section

Historical documents can also be found in the government publications section. The library is the depository for state publications and is also the only complete depository for U.S. publications in the state. Patrons can find documents from all levels of government, including out-of-state documents, on a wide range of current topics. At the same time, historical researchers can find items such as maps and reports published by the California State Department of Mines and Geology, early copies of the Governor's Budget, and reports dating back to the first governor.

### Law Library

In addition to providing current legal source materials, such as codes, statutes, court reports, local charters and ordinances, the law library also contains special collections of historical significance. The collection includes state legislative bills from 1867 to the present, and volumes of California land claim records and briefs before the courts and Board of Land Commissioners in Mexican and Spanish land grant confirmation cases.

### Braille and Talking Book Library

The Braille and Talking Book Library is a branch of the State Library that works with the Library of Congress' National Library Service for the Blind and Physically handicapped in loaning braille and talking books to Northern Californians unable to read standard print due to visual or physical limitations. Residents of Southern California are served by the Braille Institute Library in Los Angeles, which is also funded by the State Library.

### State Information and Reference Center (SIRC)

The Center provides reference assistance to its primary clientele, the legislature and state employees, and also to the public though use of materials in the reference collection, the General Collection, and materials borrowed through interlibrary loan. SIRC staff also man the Capitol Branch reference desk located on the second floor of the State Capitol Building, provide interlibrary reference, and respond to letters from California citizens referred to us from the Library of Congress. This paper will focus on the Reference Center and those special services it provides to its patrons, such as bringing new trends to their attention.

## SPECIAL TOPICS

Although the Reference Center's librarians may not be trendsetters, they can spot trends and hot topics faster than any other people I know. In the course of their work they scan thousands of journals in every discipline and assist hundreds of patrons in finding both specific and topical information. Through their daily work they become aware of issues and topics that the state government and the public are investigating.

The Reference Center recognizes and utilizes this knowledge to produce a series of publications entitled *Special Topics*. The goals of each issue are to alert patrons to an issue of current or emerging statewide interest, to provide annotated citations to representative literature on the topic, and to educate our clients about library and other resources available to them. Each and every issue has met these goals.

The first issue of the series, "Immigration: A Pacific Perspective" debuted in April of 1986. Since then, over two dozen other issues have been disseminated on an irregular basis.

The diverse range of subjects addressed include literacy, groundwater protection, child care, traffic congestion, and local government finance.

As mentioned earlier, one of the goals of *Special Topics* is to help alert patrons to concerns of statewide interest, and to assist legislative staff in their research on the topics. *Special Topics* has been able to keep in step with these research needs and issues. For example, the June 1987 issue focused on California's growing traffic congestion problem. The following month, *California Journal*, a major publication presenting analysis of state government and politics, ran an article titled "The Fear of Gridlock: Can California's Freeways be Saved From a Future of Perpetual Gridlock?" Subsequently, the Assembly Office of Research of the California Legislature published *California 2000: Gridlock in the Making, Major Issues in Transportation* in 1988.

*Special Topics* informs patrons of resources available on the topic. Both print and non-print resources are cited in the publication, as well as resources outside of the library. And every resource cited is available to our primary clientele.

The majority of items cited are articles, monographs, government publications, and periodicals, with other resources listed as appropriate. For instance, in the issue addressing groundwater protection, information of the *Enviroline* and *Environmental Law Reporter* databases, both accessible by the library, is provided. While the issue devoted to microcomputing contained information on local microcomputer user groups, and the State Microcomputer Forum.

Information resources available on various topics are not, and should not be limited to those contained within the physical boundaries of the library.

## MANAGEMENT TRENDS

Another publication series issued as a service to the library's clientele is *Management Trends*. On a monthly basis *Management Trends* brings current publications on the world of business to its reader's attention. Special emphasis is placed on management and supervision, office automation, and organizational behavior.

Approximately three dozen items are listed and briefly described each month. These items are grouped by subject categories such as desktop publishing, communication, performance appraisals, and leaders and leadership. The materials cited cover both the practical and theoretical aspects of each discipline. Two samples appear below:

> Boosting Your Career with Politics, by Jeffrey P. Davidson. In *Management World*, vol. 17, no. 5 (September/October 1988), pp. 11-13.
> Your professional future may depend upon how well you understand your company's informal power structure and how you spend your lunch hours.

> When Making That Decision, by Bernard A. Deitzer and Alan G. Kriglline. In *Management Solutions*, vol. 33, no. 11 (November 1988), pp. 3-9.
> "Decision making is a part of every supervisor or manager's job, but it is not the easiest part by any means. Faced with a tough choice, some managers find themselves paralyzed, incapable of thought or action. Understanding the decision making process can help relieve some of the tension that choosing one route over another can bring on. And following the advice offered here can help improve a manager's choices."

Preparation of *Management Trends* benefits not only the library's patrons, but staff as well. The review of current management materials keeps staff apprised of current management and supervision principles and acts as a source of continuing education. Responsibility for *Management Trends* is rotated among reference center staff.

Both *Management Trends* and *Special Topics* are distributed at no charge. State employees and libraries can subscribe to either one, or both of these series.

## LIBRARY ORIENTATIONS

Any discussion of services provided to patrons is not complete without some comment on a basic library service, library orientations. To most people, using the library is like using a computer. Both are complex systems. You can struggle to learn how to use them by yourself, or someone can instruct you in how to use them, and to make full use of their potential.

Since not all patrons are the same, neither should the orientations. The State Library tailors its orientations to the needs of each group, because an orientation given to agricultural chemical researchers is not suited for visiting high school students and vice versa. Therefore, each time an orientation is requested, staff take the following factors into consideration when planning the session: age of the group, their primary purpose for requesting the orientation, resources available at the State Library not available at their local library, methods in which they would access the State Library's resources, their familiarity with library services and research, and printed materials about the library that will be useful to them after they leave the library. Based upon these needs, staff have given orientations focusing on specific hardware and software review sources to state agency data processing personnel, orientations to genealogical resources in the library for genealogists, general overview orientations to visiting elementary school students, and a variety of other orientations.

## ONLINE SEARCH SERVICES

Most of our orientations would not be complete without some mention of the library's online search service. Integrated into the library's reference service, staff have access to over 300 databases available through DIALOG® Information Services, BRS® Technologies Inc., Mead Data Central's LEXIS/NEXIS® system, Pergamon ORBIT®, VuText®, DATATIMES, NEWSNET®, the National Library of Medicine's MEDLARS system, LEGISNET, the Council of State Government's ISIS system, RLIN, and the University of California MELVYL® system. Staff conduct online searches for state employees working on state business either upon specific request from patrons, or as needed to fulfill their information demands. There is absolutely no charge to the patron or their agency for the service since all costs are borne by the library.

The online search service is a significant component of the reference department. Each year over 3500 online subject searches are performed. And the service doesn't end once the search printout is delivered to the patron.

With their printouts patrons receive information on two other library services, interlibrary loan, and material collection. The cover letter of the search printout instructs the patron to look over the citations and highlight items desired. If the patron does not have the time to retrieve the items himself, or if it would place an inconvenience on him, he can send the marked printout to the reference center where library staff will gather, charge out, and send the materials to the patron's office. If there are items cited on the printout not held by the library, the patron can request the library borrow them for him through the interlibrary loan service. No limits are placed on the number of items gathered or the number of titles borrowed through interlibrary loan. It's important to remember that all our reference related services are geared toward fully meeting the information needs of our primary users. It would be contrary to our goal to limit the amount of information provided to our patrons.

## *MELVYL®*

With the patron in mind, the library has also stationed public access terminals connecting to the University of California's MELVYL Online Catalog throughout the library. Several years earlier the State Library and the Division of Library Automation of the University of California conducted a joint test project whereby approximately 30,000 State Library catalog records were loaded into MELVYL and terminals were placed in various public service areas. The overall patron response was overwhelmingly positive. Users enjoyed the benefits of being able to locate records online not only in the State Library, but in the vast resources of the University of California Library System as well. Subsequently, an Interagency Agreement was signed which enabled State Library current catalog records to be added to MELVYL on a monthly basis, and well as retrospective records.

At present, MELVYL terminals are located in every public service area of the library, as well as the Capitol Branch and Sutro Branch. Selected terminals will also have printers allowing patrons to print off lists of items they wish to obtain. Again, no limit is being placed on the number of citations they will be allowed to print, or the number of materials gathered.

## FUNDING SOURCES INFORMATION CENTER

As financial support for worthwhile projects continues to diminish, the library has enlarged its collection of materials on funding sources. Housed in the reference center, the Funding Sources Information Center (FSIC) is a collection of materials that provide information on all aspects of securing and managing external sources of funding. These materials include guides on proposal writing, fundraising, directories of foundations, directories of federal and private grants, directories of grants, scholarships and awards to individuals, and books on grant management, and on setting up a nonprofit corporation.

Through maintenance of the FSIC collection, it became apparent that no source adequately described grants awarded and/or administered by California State agencies and departments. To remedy this situation, reference center staff contact the various agencies on an annual basis to gather information on grants they administer. The information is compiled and published as the *Catalog of State Grants Assistance*. Copies of the catalog are available for use in the Funding Sources Information Center, and can also be purchased from the California State Library Foundation if desired.

The Funding Sources Information Center is consulted frequently by representatives of area associations and non-profit organizations seeking external funding for worthwhile projects. Library staff have also noticed an increased use of the collection by representatives of public agencies seeking additional funds to supplement their diminishing budgets. Perhaps as a sign of the nation's financial climate, use of the FSIC continues to increase with each year.

## BOOKS FROM AROUND THE WORLD

With the benefit of the end-user in mind, the State Information and Reference Center also compiles and publishes a quarterly bibliography entitled *Books From Around the World*. *Books From Around the World* focuses on the non-english materials in the State Library's collections. Each issue is devoted to materials in a specific language, such as Vietnamese, Spanish, or Arabic.

As California continues to grow more ethnically diverse, public libraries are facing greater demands for a variety of non-english materials. *Books From Around the World* provides these libraries with specific titles of non-english materials in the State Library which can be borrowed to help fulfill their patrons' needs. All non-english titles are circulated for three months.

Libraries can request materials in other languages by specific authors and titles, or by specific subjects, or by type of fiction. Mini-collections of ten to twenty-five titles per language can also be requested for use as a short-term library collection. The State Library's language collection is aimed at supplementing the non-english collections of public libraries, not replacing them.

## STATE AGENCY LIBRARY ASSISTANCE

The State Library also provides assistance to state agency personnel in developing a small library, as well as assisting existing state agency libraries in fulfilling their missions. To assist these agencies, reference staff have prepared two publications, *The Basics*, and *CAL INFO*. There is no charge to the agencies for either publication.

*The Basics* is a how-to guide written for non-professional state agency personnel who are responsible for organizing and operating a small library. The guide covers the acquisition and cataloging processes as well as circulation, reference, and interlibrary loan services. Illustrations of sample forms and a list of suggested reference materials for California agency libraries are also included in the guide. State Library Services Bureau staff also provide assistance and consultation to state agency libraries.

*CAL INFO: California Agency Libraries and Information Sources* provides librarians with information on the services of California agency libraries. Over 160 agency libraries are surveyed as to their hours, staff, and services (such as interlibrary loan, photocopying etc.). *CAL INFO* is distributed to California state agency libraries without charge. Both *CAL INFO* and *The Basics* have not been updated for several years, but will be when time permits.

## *CONCLUSION*

Although this article focuses primarily on the special services provided by the State Information and Reference Center, it should be noted that a number of special services are also provided by other departments within the State Library. For instance, the Law Library compiles and publishes the *California County Law Library Directory*, and the *California County Law Library Statistics*. The Government Publications Section publishes an index to California state publications. The Braille and Talking Book Library publishes a semi-annual newsletter in braille, and in large print. And the Library Development Services Bureau publishes the *California Library Directory*, and *California Library Statistics* among a number of other publications. The Bureau also maintains a database of automation applications in libraries.

This article has just begun to focus on the "more than just the ordinary" library services provided to its valued patrons. It can be confidently said, the California State Library provides its patrons with more than just an answer.

## REFERENCES

1. Silver, Cy. "The New State Library Annex Building (Site 5) – It's History and Features." *California State Library Foundation Bulletin*, Oct. 1988, p. 29.
2. California Education Code 19320(h).

# The Public and Bibliographic Instruction: Missed Opportunities in Creating a Positive Information Environment

Sheila S. Intner

**SUMMARY.** Since Bibliographic Instruction seems to be offered to many people using libraries, one could expect that a more knowledgeable public with a positive view of the information environment is being developed among its recipients. Who is the public for Bibliographic Instruction and what are they learning? Who is not being served and what are the implications of that failure? Can we define something called "Library Appreciation," and should it be taught to all clients before other library curricula?

A great deal of excellent literature is available that describes a wide variety of services subsumed under the rubric "Bibliographic Instruction."[1] Instructional services would appear to be ubiquitous, regardless of library type, location, or constituency. They would seem to be part of standard operating procedures throughout the academic sector as well as in forward-looking public libraries. One might begin to believe that it is virtually impossible to escape encountering Bibliographic Instruction services in the ordinary course of library use.

Since Bibliographic Instruction seems to be offered to so many people using libraries, one could expect that a more knowledgeable public is being created—indeed, has been created over the last twenty years. And, one might expect that a positive view of the information environment is being developed among its recipients, either as a primary objective or a spinoff benefit of the instructional

---

Sheila S. Intner is Associate Professor, Simmons College Graduate School of Library and Information Science, 300 The Fenway, Boston, MA 02115.

*15*

program. This paper explores some of these issues: Who is the public for Bibliographic Instruction and what are they learning? Who is not being served and what are the implications of that failure and those lost opportunities?

## LIMITING THE TERRITORY

Bibliographic Instruction takes many forms. Any discussion about it requires some definition of boundaries. Where does reference service leave off and Bibliographic Instruction begin? For one thing, almost everything a librarian does in the process of helping people find what they want in the library, which we call reference or readers' advisory services, can be construed as instruction. If I ask a reference librarian where to find biographical material about Ludwig van Beethoven, the answer I receive is an answer to a reference question. But, it could also be interpreted, technically, as Bibliographic Instruction. Certainly, if the librarian lectured a class on this subject, it would count as Bibliographic Instruction, since most of us would not think of lecturing as answering a group reference question. (At least, I am not aware of the existence of such things as class action reference questions akin to class action legal suits.) To some degree, then, Bibliographic Instruction involves imparting knowledge about library materials and services to more than one person.

Yet, whenever I talk to public librarians, the idea of one-on-one Bibliographic Instruction arises. Since adults rarely arrive in cities or towns in large groups expecting to proceed as a group with their daily lives, reference and adult services librarians working in public libraries have no counterpart to the school or academic librarians' annual encounter with entering classes. In contrast, public library reference librarians tend to deal with adults individually or, at most, in concert with a relative or a friend. Is it impossible for their efforts to be termed Bibliographic Instruction? Considered one case at a time, the answer would probably be "Yes." But, taken together, the librarian might teach many people the same lesson. If the effort is repeated for many people at various times, it does not differ materially from a group encounter in which all the people are taught simultaneously.

The element that distinguishes Bibliographic Instruction from other reference services is not so much how many people are instructed at a time or whether instruction of any sort takes place during the librarian-client interchange. Rather, it is the systematic nature of the effort to teach something — a set of principles or search strategies relating to the library, its collections or services — using predetermined methods in order to accomplish a predefined set of objectives. That is the working definition of Bibliographic Instruction to be understood throughout this article.

Using this definition, a response to my query about Beethoven that simply directs me to the biography shelves armed with the information that they are arranged alphabetically by biographee is merely an answer to a reference question. It would count as Bibliographic Instruction only if, in advance of my question, the librarian had thought about the need for and uses of biographical materials, devised objectives for biographical searching, created a lesson teaching search processes and relevant sources, and then, used it to inform me. I might expect to learn much more than the location of shelves where the library housed its biographies. The lesson would be repeated for any member of the public who inquired about biographies or related subjects.

This raises an important point about Bibliographic Instruction. Most of the literature focuses on what is being done in schools — particularly in colleges and universities, but also in elementary and secondary schools — to train library users. Elementary and secondary school libraries have a great deal in common with college and university libraries. The library is used for similar purposes, at least at the upper grade levels, and the same kinds of user problems often must be resolved. Some institutions include classes in library skills, too. These may be geared to any grade level, from K-3 to senior high school and beyond. The primary difference between lower and higher educational institutions (and these terms are merely used to identify, not to impart any degree of importance), seems to arise in relation to Bibliographic Instruction for faculty and post-baccalaureate researchers. Since these are differences that might apply to some colleges also, they are ignored in this article. Anything that applies to any part of the academic world is taken here to apply to all school situations generally, regardless of student ages or grade levels.

The other term that needs definition is "the public." The public is such an amorphous entity that it is almost impossible to discuss in any meaningful way without defining it. It is a great mistake to define public carelessly as, for example, anyone who uses the library (a definition I believe is not untypical and is consistent with the overly general notion of libraries having "users" without further specification). The idea that the public bears a single image — many individuals, but all virtually identical — is one that causes all sorts of problems, since few academic, public, or school libraries serve homogeneous client groups. Instead, there are many groups of users, each having different needs, purposes, problems, and status in the eyes of the library's administration. Important distinctions may be made between the primary and auxiliary user groups of a library. How librarians define the groups — broadly or narrowly — and how they interpret the library's responsibility toward each group is likely to determine who, if anyone, will receive Bibliographic Instruction, the form that instruction takes, and what kinds of information are presented in instructional sessions.

## WHO IS THE PUBLIC
## FOR BIBLIOGRAPHIC INSTRUCTION?

The knee-jerk reaction to the question "Who is the public for Bibliographic Instruction?" is the library's primary user group. Certainly, this is true in elementary and secondary schools, where the primary user group is the student body, who are the beneficiaries of virtually all programs of Bibliographic Instruction that might be provided. Formal instructional contacts with other groups in the school environment — administrators, faculty, or parents — are rarely described, although they undoubtedly exist in some places.

In colleges and universities, there may be two or three primary user groups: students and faculty; or, sometimes separately designated undergraduates, graduate students and faculty. While administrative personnel in these institutions also might have all the usual borrowing privileges of a student or faculty member, serving them is rarely considered an integral part of the libraries' mission and, thus, they are not included in the primary clientele. Bibliographic Instruction for both (or all) of the primary groups is often supported and addressed. But, it is also possible that students will be targeted for the instructional programs, while faculty will receive different kinds of services introducing them to library collections and services ranging from information kits placed in their mailboxes to personal visits from librarians specializing in the appropriate disciplines — and very little more.

Public libraries, who usually designate residents as their primary clienteles, usually do not have formal Bibliographic Instruction for adults. It is children who typically receive whatever instructional services are provided. Children may come in groups from local schools, brought on field trips by their teachers, or in ones and twos, brought by their parents. In either case, it is likely to be the children's staff members who handle their instruction. Information service or reference staff are more likely to handle adult Bibliographic Instruction, if any is provided.

## WHAT ARE THEY LEARNING?

Bibliographic Instruction comprises many individual types of services, but they can be grouped into three categories: Library skills; sources and literature; and, learning about the library in which they take place.

### Library Skills

Library skills curricula traditionally have centered on bibliographic searching and information retrieval systems, unraveling the organizational core that underlies all library operations. Library skills include searching the catalog effectively and deciphering the catalog entries, getting around in whatever classification system is used to shelve library materials, and using indexes to find information in periodicals and other kinds of documents. The advent of computer-based information systems, however, caused something of a dilemma for Bibliographic Instruction, and trends in instructional services relating to computer-based systems have shifted more than once over the years since their arrival in libraries.

Retrieving information from computerized indexes in online mode — whether these were a library network union catalog, the local library catalog or a multi-database reference system such as DIALOG — added the need to teach use of the computer to the traditional retrieval skills. Operation of new online systems was so complex and technical that access to them tended to be limited to a tiny group of initiates. The library profession was immobilized for a time between two seemingly incompatible demands: The natural inclination to embrace online systems and to teach the public how to use them without a librarian's assistance (much as they had always done with indexes in book form)[2] and the inability to pay for sufficient time online to experiment and teach, or, in some instances, even to become experts themselves.

During the decade of the 1970's some predicted that computers would replace human librarians, but, before 1980 it seemed that computers were not only not doing so, they were creating a new demand for expert services. Ordinary people — even ordinary librarians — could not walk up to a DIALOG or OCLC terminal and perform a search. One had to undergo a training course to learn how to search online and, because online searching was costly, the value received for search time had to be maximized. Libraries began charging fees for online search services and, because the fees rarely covered costs completely, simultaneously devised methods of minimizing the use of online systems. Librarians forgot about teaching people how to use online indexes and, instead, began performing searches on their behalf. The mediated online search began to render the public utterly dependent on librarians, while the notion of teaching computer literacy as a library skill started to take on a desperate kind of importance, especially to those who found the situation untenable.

But, beginning in 1980, the microcomputer with its focus on direct use by ordinary people burst on the information market. It did not take commercial index publishers very long to appreciate that microcomputer-based indexes were affordable not only by tens of thousands of libraries, but by millions of individuals, and they responded accordingly.

An important and appealing part of the magic of computerized indexes was their ability to help searchers accomplish something easily and quickly. Publishers realized that the more enjoyable the search and the more efficient and satisfying the system appeared, the more it would be used. This enormous market potential, aided and abetted by spreading ownership and use of personal computers, advances in computer hardware, software, and telecommunications, and inexorable drops in prices, motivated publishers to develop self help strategies that eliminated the need to teach anyone how to use their systems. User-friendly end user searching might eventually eliminate some library services and render certain components of current library skills programs obsolete.[3] The dire predictions might yet come true, at least in part.

### Sources and Literature

Search tools to which the library client often is introduced in Bibliographic Instruction sessions are, primarily, reference works ranging from bibliographies and indexes to encyclopedias, directories, and dictionaries. Sources for bibliographic citations that lead to other materials are most important, hence there is emphasis on materials that provide them: bibliographies, bio-bibliographies, indexes, and encyclopedias. Answer books, e.g., atlases, almanacs, dictionaries, and directories, are important, too, but are usually distinguished as "ready reference" sources, not as aids to further research.

Important literature—dissertations, periodicals, treatises and literary works that comprise primary and secondary research material—may be covered, too, particularly if the subject areas covered in an instructional session are limited to a single discipline or subdiscipline. Then, there is time to discuss the patterns of literature of that field, noting landmark works or particularly useful and scholarly works for the novice researcher. But, the location of periodical indexes and periodical volumes/issues are almost always covered, since these comprise a valuable source-literature system.

Librarians teaching more general sessions on literature searching probably do well to avoid discussing individual titles, since few of them would be of interest to the majority of their students. One of my library science students described exercises used in her college's Bibliographic Instruction program in which each student in a class being taught was encouraged to find three titles related to an individually-chosen topic and report the method by which they were located. The librarian teaching the class then evaluated the search process for each student in terms of what titles they found and how they found them. Perhaps such customized instruction is less rare than I suspect, but no surveys confirm or deny my opinion that it is unusual.

### Learning About the Individual Library

For a great many librarians, Bibliographic Instruction means giving guided tours of the library, pointing out the reference department ("Here is our Information Desk . . .") and some of its most popular resources ("The *Reader's Guide* is kept on that desk over there . . .")and mentioning otherwise invisible materials and services ("You'll find older issues of some of our periodicals on microfilm in the Media Center, behind the football field on the other side of campus . . ."). Clearly, one must begin somewhere and the library tour is a good first step for any newcomer.

Acknowledging the importance of introductions to one's buildings, physical arrangement of collections, and location of service points, however, should not mean confusing them with *Bibliographic* Instruction—there is nothing bibliographic about guided tours.[4]

Qualifying more accurately as Bibliographic Instruction, perhaps, are introductions to the library's catalogs and other finding tools. Sometimes such introductions are part of guided tours. ("Here's the catalog . . . It lists everything in the library [*sic*.] and it can be searched by author, title, and subject." This remark, which I witnessed as a participant in a library tour, was accompanied by a wave of the librarian's hand that constituted the total information about the catalog imparted to the group.)

Sometimes use of the catalog is taught in separate instructional sessions offered to classes or smaller groups, or, occasionally, to individuals. It seems to me that there is greater likelihood that useful information about what is *not* in the catalog, what idiosyncratic practices are followed by the library in cataloging, filing, and shelving, and what alternative finding tools are available will be discussed in an instructional session that is not part of a guided tour, and, therefore, that it is a more valuable form of instruction.

Instruction in the use of the library's public access computer systems may be added to other library-specific information. ("Public access computing" — a generic term — was deliberately chosen to describe both computer-based library systems and systems available in the library that support general computing, which might include statistical computation, word processing, database storage and management, etc.) A goodly proportion of recent literature in Bibliographic Instruction describes methods of employing computers instead of librarians to teach traditional library skills and/or other components of the instructional program. When one considers how many library clients can benefit from bibliographic instruction and how few librarians there are to furnish it, this seems like a promising solution.

## MISSED OPPORTUNITIES AND THEIR IMPACT

Missed opportunities fall into two categories: people who are not being served by programs of Bibliographic Instruction; and curricula that are not being taught in existing programs.

### Who Is Not Receiving Bibliographic Instruction

It is easy to neglect whole categories of users in designing Bibliographic Instruction programs. Even if the neglect is unavoidable, laid at the door of skimpy budgets, inadequate staffing, or the demands of more pressing problems with higher priorities, it is there, nevertheless. I suspect the largest and most important of the neglected categories are the people who do not use the library at all, the non-users, but they are not alone. In many academic and public libraries, staff users are left out. In school library media centers, faculty tend to be ignored. In virtually all libraries, the public is equated with the primary user group, whatever that is, and all secondary or auxiliary groups get short shrift, although there are some notable exceptions.[5]

Clearly, Bibliographic Instruction fails non-users and others whose secondary status places them outside the realm of concern. It may even fail the library's primary users. Reaching everyone in large universities is not easy. There are enormous logistic problems in providing every new student with one general tour, let alone trying to reach each of them individually with customized follow-ups and instructional sessions. There are transfer students who are uncomfortable being grouped with those from lower classes. If instructional sessions are optional, there are those who fail to exercise the option. Class-related Bibliographic Instruction sessions only reach those who take particular classes and faculty are rarely required to include them. An informal survey of one of my beginning cataloging classes revealed that, of the twenty-one master's degree students, four had never encountered Bibliographic Instruction and two more received their instruction solely from their parents.[6]

Faculty members, although a much smaller group, are difficult to reach. Some of them anticipate having library tours or hearing about searching or online services with as much relish as being herded to their last judgments, while some feel that their very attendance at an instructional session or a tour is a public display of their lack of knowledge.

But, the largest group of people not being reached surely must be adults who use public libraries. They must ask for help (not an easy thing for many of us) and librarians must be willing and able to do a great deal more than respond with easy answers (not an easy thing, either). Bibliographic Instruction is not integrated into the public library environment and no groundswell of need is discussed in the public library literature as it is in academic and school library literatures. The job must be done at earlier stages in these people's lives if they are to be encouraged to ask for instruction when they use public libraries as adults.[7]

## What Is Not Being Taught

The most important curriculum not being taught is Library Appreciation — an overview of the information culture, its principles, components, structures, and systems, and the role of libraries as an essential element in it.

In many elementary schools and even secondary schools, there are no librarians, so it may be classroom teachers who explain use of the library to students, not librarians with professional training in bibliographic principles and systems. Without detracting from classroom teachers' knowledge and skills, this could impact negatively on what is taught to younger children as well as how effectively it is taught.

In colleges and universities, it is too easy to dismiss the importance of introductions to the library and assign them to whoever happens to be handy, not more importantly occupied, or merely willing. Certainly, even the most routine assignment should be taken seriously, conducted by knowledgeable staff members, in carefully thought out patterns, and arranged to cover highlights with suggestions for more specific follow-ups. The library tour should be considered strictly a warm-up,[8] not the whole show, and real instructional sessions should follow it. (Regarding the introductory tour, my students tell me they generally remember only one or two of the dozens of things they are shown. Considering that my college has a small and relatively centralized library, this bodes ill for larger institutions with decentralized collections and services.)

## LIBRARY APPRECIATION: AN OPPORTUNITY TO CREATE A POSITIVE INFORMATION ENVIRONMENT

An esteemed colleague once made a large audience of library professionals rock with laughter by relating that his daughter called her undergraduate Music Appreciation course "Clapping for Credit." Behind the laughter he provoked, however, was a serious theme: Before students can begin to understand music, an appreciation for the subject must be created. At best, Music Appreciation can whet the appetites of fledgling musicians, musicologists, or music lovers. At worst, it might help non-musical persons enjoy music more than they did previously by imparting an overview of musical history and tradition, compositional and performance techniques, and by exposing them to a group of much-beloved pieces.

Is Bibliographic Instruction an opportunity to create a more appreciative library audience (or, one could say, a more positive and knowledgeable view of the information environment) in much the same way that Music Appreciation coursework endeavors to do for the musical audience? Can we define something called Library Appreciation and should it be taught as the first part of Bibliographic Instruction? Three elements figure importantly in drawing an analogy between Music Appreciation and Bibliographic Instruction as an opportunity to teach Library Appreciation: First, emphasizing an overview approach; second, establishing links between theory and practice; and, third, earning credit (this last element figures solely in the academic world).

### Emphasizing an Overview Approach

Bibliographic Instruction programs tend to have tightly focused, practical objectives, e.g., searching a periodical index to find relevant articles for a paper, then locating the articles in the library. There is very little time, much to do, and very few people to do the job. Evaluation of the program might be based on how many people are served, not the quality of the service, so the idea is to make the numbers look good (in such an institution it is better to give one hour of Bibliographic Instruction to 1,000 students in which they learn very little than to teach 500 several useful skills that might take three or four hours, instead).

It is difficult to orient Bibliographic Instruction toward the Big Picture. The difference between "Appreciation" or "Survey" courses on the one hand, and other, more specific ones on the other, however, is the attempt of the former to provide an overview that covers an entire field. Without being exposed to an overview approach, it is hard to appreciate much more about learning how to locate a periodical article than that it is useful to prepare a term paper or to fulfill a course exercise. Beginning, instead, by learning how information is generated, disseminated, and used, how earlier works become the basis for future research and artistry, how information can be structured and restructured as well as how knowledge and information overlap, but are not identical, gives one a different perspective on locating that journal article and its functioning in the dynamic process of human intellectual activity. The economics and the ethics of information use need to be explored, too, as do the implications of different types of information policy. All of these are pertinent to discuss in a Library Appreciation course, but time-consuming and impractical to cover in an ordinary Bibliographic Instruction session.

## Linking Theory and Practice

Analyzing practice to see how it relates to underlying principles and how the theoretical structures on which information systems are based ultimately result in useful products and services also should be part of Library Appreciation. Is it useful to examine the information infrastructure? Surely, to use it intelligently, one must understand what it is, how it is built, how it operates, and what problems are encountered. There is power in understanding how systems work as well as the potential for greater control over one's interactions with them, greater precision and more effective use of those systems — something akin to what is gained from knowing about the physical nature of electricity, even for students who will not become electrical engineers or physicists.

Allowing students to assume that periodical indexes grow on library shelves is as uninstructive as allowing them to assume that canned vegetables grow on supermarket shelves. We strive to enlighten them on the latter; why not the former?

## Earning Credit

Humans, being the imperfect creatures they are, are able to consider some alternative action that is clearly beneficial and can improve their lot, and fail to choose it. It is no accident that Music Appreciation was dubbed Clapping for *Credit*. Few undergraduates elect to clap for nothing (or, only for the good it might do their souls). I submit that without the carrot of credit or the stick of a (non-credit) requirement for graduation (such as many colleges and universities have done for physical education courses in order to avoid giving academic credit for playing tennis, volleyball, golf, etc.), few undergraduates would elect a course in Library Appreciation, Bibliographic Instruction, or whatever else we decided to call it, even though the course might afford them enormous power over the information environment in which they live and work. Being good for them is not enough.

When East Carolina University in Greenville, North Carolina,

offered courses in bibliographic skills for credit, they were successful in attracting students.[9] Nor were they alone.[10] The only people
who need no other motivation than improving their intellectual lot
to be attracted to the Bibliographic Instruction program are certain
adults using the public library, who can have a variety of personal
reasons for wanting to understand information systems better. The
rest of the universe of the uninformed need more tangible benefits
from the opportunities being offered than promises of undefined
future power.

To be worth academic credits, however, a course of instruction
should attempt to do more than point out the locations of indexes or
demonstrate how to search the library's computerized catalog. Such
a course should explore the infrastructure of the contemporary information world, the theory and principles of information storage
and retrieval systems, and, perhaps, even information policies, economics, and ethical uses of information. There are many important
and useful topics that might be covered and, in addition to learning
the best way to search a periodical index, students should learn the
principles by which indexes are organized generally as well as how
and why they are published and maintained. In fact, if elementary,
secondary and undergraduate students were exposed to the larger
information world, some might be tempted to pursue a career in
library/information service themselves, an auxiliary benefit of no
small significance.

## CONCLUSIONS

Bibliographic Instruction rarely is designed to introduce library
clients to the whole world of information. Often it is directed almost
exclusively toward local concerns, such as where specific books,
journals, or terminals are located and how to access them. An appreciation for bibliographic principles and systems is not stressed.
More often than not, if a specific exercise is taught, its applicability
to other sources or other systems is not mentioned. This loss of
opportunities to create a more knowledgeable and appreciative library audience — one that understands that real librarians do not
stamp dates in books or admonish people to be quiet, but are experts
who can furnish links to a larger information environment — rever-

berates negatively throughout our society. Lack of more integrative Bibliographic Instruction puts library clients at a strong disadvantage as they move from one library to another. Lack of the Library Appreciation component fails to encourage people to turn to librarians for expert advice in the sophisticated information environment in which we live. Instead, non-bibliographic and overly specific instructional encounters seem to teach clients that they should fend for themselves in libraries while presenting libraries as simple systems.

Those who go unserved by little or no Bibliographic Instruction may end up perceiving libraries as unrelated to their needs, desires, and concerns, much as those who have no exposure to or understanding of music or art have little personal interest in concert halls or galleries and museums. Libraries might be thought of as "good" for others, as worthy-but-dispensable cultural attractions in their communities, but not as places where people like themselves can find out whatever they want or need to know, where ideas abound, and where they can plumb the length and breadth of humanity's intellectual heritage. Not only is this a loss for the people; it is a fundamental loss for us as library professionals, and for our libraries.

## REFERENCES

1. Articles and regular features on Bibliographic Instruction appear both in scholarly periodicals, such as *The Reference Librarian*, *RQ*, *College & Research Libraries*, *The Journal of Academic Librarianship*, *Journal of Youth Services*, etc., and the profession's mass media, e.g., in *American Libraries*, *Wilson Library Bulletin*, *Library Journal*, *School Library Journal*, etc. Many, if not most, of these articles and columns describe some successful, innovative instructional project, program, or policy being implemented somewhere. A modest number of monographs and a wealth of association-or institution-generated pamphlets, kits, and booklets appear each year that add to a rapidly growing body of Bibliographic Instruction literature.

2. See, for example, Linda Friend, "Independence at the Terminal: Training Student End Users to Do Online Literature Searching," *Journal of Academic Librarianship* 11 (1985):136-41.

3. Changes in the role of libraries and instructional relations with library clients are explored in Alan E. Guskin et al., "Library Future Shock: The Micro-

computer Revolution and the New Role of the Library," *College & Research Libraries* 45 (May 1984):177-83.

4. Association of College and Research Libraries, Bibliographic Instruction Section, Continuing Education Committee, *Organizing and Managing a Library Instruction Program: Checklists; Preconference [at] Southern Methodist University, Dallas Texas, June 21-23, 1979* (Chicago: The Association, 1980), pp. 2, 6. To its credit, the committee did not include library tours in its initial list of forms of Library (i.e., Bibliographic) Instruction; but, library tours and handouts of floor plans and handbooks (which tend to focus on borrowing rules and lists of services) do appear in a later section covering assessment of students' previous Library Instruction experience. There is no way of knowing if the absence of tours on the first list was merely an oversight and if their inclusion on the second was acknowledgement of the reality that tours constitute the whole Bibliographic Instruction program in some places; or whether both were unintentional, random occurrences.

5. The most notable exception that comes to mind are school children, especially from private schools, in public libraries.

6. Sheila S. Intner, "Interfaces: The Self-Service Library: Implications for Bibliographic Instruction," *Technicalities* 6 (Mar. 1986):13.

7. Ibid, p. 13-14. The same survey showed that nine students first received Bibliographic Instruction while they were in elementary school, five while in junior high, one in senior high, and only two as college undergraduates. (This includes the two who were taught by their parents.) A few commented that subsequent experiences reinforced their initial encounters, but most indicated that early instruction faded and their current knowledge came from job-related experiences.

8. Tours guided personally by a librarian are not the only method of showing newcomers around the premises. Other methods I have seen in use are slide-tape shows, self-guided tours in which the person uses a map with brief commentaries added for various service points, a sound cassette that directs the person from place to place offering commentary at each stopping point — this is very popular in art museums — and sets of color-coded footsteps temporarily placed throughout the library at the beginning of the year to direct new patrons to reference (red), serials (blue), circulation (orange), book stacks (yellow), and nonbook media (green).

9. Linda B. Langley, "The Effects of a Credit Course in Bibliographic Instruction," *Technicalities* 7 (Nov. 1987):3-7.

10. See, for example, Mignon S. Adams and Jacqueline M. Morris, *Teaching Library Skills for Academic Credit* (Phoenix, Arizona: Oryx Press, 1985); and Rae Haws et al., "Survey of Faculty Attitudes towards a Basic Library Skills Course," *C&RL News* (Mar. 1989):201-204, which describes the required credit-bearing course in library skills at Iowa State University.

# Providing Reference Assistance for Machine-Readable Materials: The Library of Congress Completes a One-Year Pilot

John Kimball, Jr.
Suzanne Thorin
Linda Arret

**SUMMARY.** In July, 1988, the Library of Congress established a one-year pilot Machine-Readable Collections Reading Room as part of its overall effort to acquire, organize, provide bibliographic control and make available to researchers machine-readable materials, both current and archival. The reference assistance required in this reading room has been significantly different from that provided in other general reading rooms in the Library of Congress. This article gives an overview of the activities in the pilot reading room and the kinds of reference encounters that have taken place there.

## INTRODUCTION

The Machine-Readable Collections Reading Room (MRCRR) was established as a one-year pilot in July 1988 in the General Reading Rooms Division at the Library of Congress. This pilot reading room has been one component of a comprehensive effort to acquire, organize, provide bibliographic control and make available to researchers materials in machine-readable formats, including microcomputer software programs and information or data files is-

---

John Kimball, Jr. is Head of the Automation and Reference Collections Section, Suzanne Thorin is Acting Chief of the General Reading Rooms Division, and Linda Arret is Automation Specialist, all at the Library of Congress, Washington, DC 20540.

sued on microcomputer, compact, or video discs. The content of the materials may be executable programs, such as those for word processing or database management, or data, such as encyclopedias, articles, indexes and abstracts. Access to mainframe or mini-computer programs or data or to commercial and other online systems has not been provided. (Many machine-readable titles used in the course of reference are also found at reference desks in other Library of Congress reading rooms; in some cases, the MRCRR will have retrospective editions or duplicate copies.)

Although the Library of Congress has been acquiring machine-readable materials since the early 1980's, it was only with the establishment of this reading room that these materials were made available to researchers. The reference staff, in addition to providing assistance in the reading room, have helped to establish collection development guidelines, assisted in establishing bibliographic control of machine-readable materials, and developed service policies and security procedures.

Reference staff assist researchers in identifying machine-readable titles, as well as other print resources such as articles, reviews, manuals, and industry studies. Users may view and work with microcomputer software only for research purposes, including comparing titles for similar applications, reviewing the different versions of a title, and examining help screens and tutorials. Personal use of microcomputer software and hardware, such as for creating one's own bibliography or writing reports, is not permitted. Reference sources on CD-ROM, such as encyclopedias, are available for consultation in the same manner one would use printed materials, to locate information. Only staff handle and install machine-readable titles.

The MRCRR, which has been housed in a temporary area due to renovation construction, has had five workstations in its pilot stage: four Compaq stations (IBM-compatible) and one Macintosh with a Sony videodisc player and monitor attached. Two of the Compaq stations also have Hitachi CD-ROM drives. Printers include Epson, Hewlett-Packard, and Apple LaserWriter.

During the pilot year of operation only IBM-compatible and Macintosh titles were able to be reviewed on the machines, but titles for other machines are being collected, and researchers may consult the manuals or other printed sources that accompany them.

## BUILDING THE COLLECTIONS

The Library of Congress collects machine-readable titles by purchase and, in addition, copyright regulations are in the process of being changed to bring machine-readable formats into conformance with print materials for deposit or registration. In the future, machine-readable titles published with a copyright notice will be required to be deposited in the Copyright Office and hence will be available for addition to the Library's own collections.

To create a core collection of microcomputer programs for the MRCRR, copies of more than four dozen items identified as industry leaders and expected to receive frequent use were purchased. These titles represent a variety of subjects and applications including: bibliography preparation, communications, database management, desktop publishing, education, graphics, integrated systems, project management, reference, spreadsheets, statistics, utilities, windowing, and word processing. A collection of CD-ROM format encyclopedias, dictionaries, directories, and periodical indexes is also being developed. Over 1,000 additional titles covering a range of applications and including formats compatible with IBM and Macintosh, as well as other hardware systems, were consolidated from other areas of the Library and are now stored in book stacks near the reading room. A print reference collection, including general reference works, third-party manuals for specific titles, industry directories, over twenty journals about the microcomputer and software industry, and a file of articles, reviews and trend studies, is also found in the reading room.

## PROVIDING BIBLIOGRAPHIC CONTROL

The Special Materials Cataloging Division, with assistance from MRCRR staff, creates catalog records for the machine-readable titles in the collection. The descriptive cataloging rules being followed are found in the revised Chapter 9 (Computer Files) of the second edition of the Anglo-American Cataloging Rules (AACR2).

For subject access, catalogers use terms from the Library's subject authority file. Catalog records are created through a microcomputer database management program, and researchers consult the catalog either online or in a printed version. The catalog records for machine-readable titles will be entered into the Library's mainframe online catalog as soon as the format for these materials is available. These records will then be searchable on terminals throughout the Library.

## DUTIES AND RESPONSIBILITIES
## OF THE REFERENCE LIBRARIANS

The Machine-Readable Collections Reading Room has been staffed by an automation specialist and three reference librarians in a sequence of three details of four months each. Early on, it became very clear that providing reference service for machine-readable materials required a whole new level of training, experience, and knowledge, with the responsibilities and duties falling into three categories: (1) knowledge of hardware and software; (2) developing of both the collection of machine-readable titles and print reference works; and (3) providing reference assistance.

*Knowledge of Hardware and Software*: The three reference librarians who were detailed to the MRCRR had been on the staff of the Library for a number of years. Although each person had received formal training in library schools in the pre-microcomputer days, they not only had enough knowledge to operate word processing programs to prepare responses to reference inquiries, research reports, and bibliographies but, in addition, were thoroughly familiar with machine-readable reference tools and had taken courses in microcomputers. We found, however, that a considerable amount of technical knowledge about the operation of microcomputers and peripheral equipment, operating systems, microcomputer application programs, and CD-ROM publications was necessary for anyone to function effectively and comfortably in the MRCRR, and it took some time for a level of comfort to be reached. The integration of complex hardware and software into the everyday procedures of the reading room has required both considerable initial technical expertise and rapid continuing growth in the technical matters.

*Collection Development*: Developing the software and CD-ROM collection, as well as a concomitant print reference collection, has been a demanding task. Identifying, ordering, processing, organizing, and storing machine-readable materials is a major project in and of itself. Particularly when building a collection from the ground up, the reference librarians, who also serve as recommending officers, have spent a considerable amount of time in collection development in addition to their reference duties. Technical support staff found that existing acquisitions procedures for print materials needed to be modified and enhanced for machine-readable works.

*Providing Reference Assistance*: Most, if not all, of our users, have been self-motivated in that they do not come to the MRCRR to fulfill a task assigned by others. In addition, most have been knowledgeable of microcomputers, though not necessarily about the applications or titles sought. Their questions tend to be precise and direct. This does not, however, necessarily result in a quicker, more effective, or more efficient interview, though it may. Especially with software, users are generally not searching for facts, concepts, and/or opinions, but rather they are searching for the capabilities of the product: What can this software do? How can I use it for my purposes? Consequently, the librarian and the user are not working together to develop a search strategy as would be done with an online catalog or other general reference or research question; instead, the interaction becomes a joint venture of exploration and discovery, with both the librarian and the user examining what software capabilities the user needs and then reviewing which capabilities exist with which titles.

Whereas, with a search strategy for a typical reference question, the user's realization of a focus for a project or inquiry represents a major leap to independence in the process, a focus is often harder to come by when software is the subject. This is the nature of the industry and the material, the industry being new and changeable and the material dynamic and interactive.

### Change in Scope of the Interview

The scope of assistance offered in the MRCRR has led to an interesting overlap between the traditions of the reference interview and bibliographic instruction. For staff, the reference encounter has been unlike the typical exchange in LC's other general reading rooms (such as the Main and Social Science reading rooms), and neither does the exchange altogether resemble what the librarians in special reading rooms, e.g., music or rare book, experience. What appears to be happening is that, especially with software, the reference interview often evolves into an instruction session where the librarian is learning while at the same time assisting and instructing the user. In the case of data, regardless of medium (floppy or optical disk), the librarian needs to offer more instructional assistance with an index or encyclopedia in electronic format than for the same source in a print edition. In both instances (software and data), the obvious and expected new demands on the reference librarian have shown a twist that we did not predict.

Additionally, it seemed to us that a room devoted to machine-readable materials would present an environment with a specific focus and, therefore, give enhanced opportunities to meet a user's needs during a reference interview; however, though machine-readable materials have a uniform characteristic in that they all require use of a microcomputer, the variety between and among applications is so astonishing that the focus can be dispersed. Though a typical reference interview pattern occasionally occurs (clarifying the question, translating the question into a form compatible with the collection resources, determining the amount of information needed, and deciding which sources to consult), the exchange rarely ends there.

The typical reference interview does not go far enough. It may be even more important than we expected to ask the user why or for what purpose an application or specific title is sought since it is often possible to find the features sought in unexpected places. It is not enough for the librarian to connect the user with a software title; in many instances, the reference librarian has had to work with the user to discover how a program operates and what its major functions are.

In the MRCRR, the librarian has tended to be a more active consultant than in most exchanges in a normal reference arena and even more active than when assisting users with the LC online catalog. Ironically, even though the MRCRR is explicitly described as not being a site where staff train users in all kinds of microcomputer applications, training occurs in the room constantly. This applies to both software and optical sources. Though we expected to offer ready reference and quick assistance, e.g., installing and trouble-shooting software and basic but elementary instructions to get started on a CD-ROM title, we did not imagine how much a reference librarian would be learning in the course of instructing.

This new situation places a different responsibility on the librarian. Though there are studies exploring librarian-user interaction in the typical reference environment and a single user's interaction with microcomputer programs, e.g., the effect of windows and color on menu choice, there appears to be very little written about the interaction between a user searching for capabilities and the librarian assisting that user.

### CD-ROMs

With CD-ROMs, the well-known lack of retrieval and display standards represents only one characteristic that has implications for instruction. The scope of a CD-ROM title is often very different from its print counterpart, at times combining several print publications into one CD-ROM and at other times eliminating earlier year coverage as later years are added. We know from catalog use studies that learning and remembering the scope of a file or system is a major problem for users. A librarian very familiar with a print reference source may have available in that source only a few modes of access to learn and impart; the same source on a CD-ROM usually provides greatly increased access. Especially with CD-ROMs, the MRCRR librarians have felt the need and desire to provide basic instruction with simple and brief printed documentation in nearby flip charts, as we have done to a much greater extent over the years with LC's online catalog.

### Software

For CD-ROMs, the instruction still remains the traditional "how to use" and "how to find information with" a specific title, but software presents more intriguing challenges. It is common to see a librarian sitting next to a user at a workstation, poring over manuals, guide cards, and templates together, in an effort to discover the capabilities of a title or to escape from an error loop. Ideally, a librarian should be fluent in all the titles in this collection, a desire not typically experienced when working with books. However, time has not permitted this knowledge, and we imagine that even with more staff, the nature of the materials would not permit ready fluency. Our users, being knowledgeable about machine-readable materials, have been sensitive and understanding about our own struggles to learn and then to teach. Without having intended that it be so, we are instructing in a way perhaps analogous to teaching basic reading and writing skills in a language we are learning as we teach, a language that, itself, is fluid. In sum, though the typical reference exchange also occurs in the MRCRR, with users consulting print serials or the vertical files, the exchange between users and librarians relating to machine-readable items is more complex with the initial interview being multifarious in its directions and sliding easily into bibliographic instruction where patron and librarian work as partners.

# Anger in the Library: Defusing Angry Patrons at the Reference Desk (and Elsewhere)

## Rhea Joyce Rubin

**SUMMARY.** Based on one of her most popular workshops, Rubin discusses the rise in displays of anger at the library and offers practical tips on how to calm the irate patron. She addresses the problem of "anger fallout" onto the library staff member involved and suggests coping methods both for individuals and libraries as administrative entities. In her workshops, participants can try out various techniques and practice new approaches. Rubin states that the tips in the article are just a starting point and suggests both further reading (a bibliography is appended) and lots of practice!

Why do people come to the library and scream at staff? Why does a wait in line, an unavailable book, an overdue fine cause such disproportionate anger? If it's any comfort, the library is not the only place normal members of the public lose their tempers.

## UNCONTROLLED ANGER ON THE RISE

Incidents of uncontrolled anger are on the rise in public places throughout America. Social scientists have many theories as to the causes of increasing rudeness and violence.[1] Psychologists claim that we have successfully curbed most expressions of anger in our family and interpersonal lives, forcing people under stress to seek

Rhea Joyce Rubin is with Rubin Consulting, 5860 Heron Drive, Oakland, CA 94618.

*39*

out opportunities to vent their frustrations. Sociologists suggest that former civic outlets for expressing outrage — such as civil right marches, anti-war demonstrations, and labor union pickets — are muted now. Again, stressful individuals must find other ways to express their frustrations. The safest arenas to do this are in anonymous situations with strangers (such as library employees, bank tellers, and grocery clerks). And many social critics cite the growth of the "me generation" — with its sense of entitlement and its need for immediate gratification — as the reason for uncontrolled anger in response to minor frustrations.[2]

Whatever the societal causes for anger in the library, we must find ways to defuse the angry patron, cope with our own anger at being a target, and develop procedures to reduce the number of angry confrontations at our reference and circulation desks.

## DEFUSING THE ANGRY PATRON

In order to defuse an angry patron, we must understand what anger is and is not. First and foremost, anger is not a rational response to a situation. Instead, anger is a primitive protective mechanism. When under stress, a "fight or flight" response is triggered. This is a series of involuntary physiological reactions which prepare us to run or to fight — but not to think. Sugar-enriched blood is pumped to the limbs (away from the brain), heart rate doubles, bronchial tubes tighten making it harder to breath, muscles tense, and the digestive system shuts down. As one researcher puts it, rage is a "Biological mechanism gone bonkers . . . a cultural malfunction."[3]

A person in this state cannot think rationally. Cannot. This is why the librarian's natural reaction — to give information — is inappropriate with an irate patron. We must calm the angry person before presenting rational solutions.

Another fact to put our habitual responses into perspective is that anger is a secondary emotion. That is, anger is developed in response to another (invisible) emotion. Common primary feelings are fear of loss of privilege, power, or prestige; embarrassment; or pain. When we see anger in a patron, it often is masking a sense of decreased trust or self-esteem. So the common reactions of being defensive and finding someone or something (often the computer) to blame are counter-productive. Instead, by making a patron feel valuable and by showing that the library is to be trusted, we can lower his/her anger.

### The First Minute

In an exchange with an upset patron, the first minute is most important. If we can smile, call him/her by name if possible, and give some genial greeting, we can head off a potential problem. Whoever speaks first sets the tone for the conversation. By being friendly and as personal as possible we are showing the patron that we value her/him and that we are not defensive. This is important, because defensive responses increase anger which increases defensiveness in an upward spiral. By speaking first we also allow the patron a moment to calm down, to let the blood flow back to the brain so that rational thought is a possibility. This is effective too because the patron who comes into the library angry is ready to do battle and expects a fight; s/he will be surprised by a friendly greeting.

If the patron is not angry until well into your exchange, these tips can be adapted. Smile and use the person's name. Buy some cooling off time by asking a question or making a supportive comment. And avoid being defensive. This is easier said than done since most people personalize anger directed at them. Sometimes it helps to ask ourselves "Is s/he angry at me or am I just a handy warm body?" Defensiveness shows itself both in words and in non-verbal language. Watch out for crossed arms, hands on hips, pointing fingers, standing above a seated patron, and rapid fire speech. Whenever possible, keep a quiet body with calm breathing and speak slightly more slowly and quietly than usual.

### Listen Sympathetically

Next we must allow the person to state the complaint and vent the anger. Try that old advice: count to ten before responding. While listening, show the patron that you are paying attention and understanding the situation. This can be done by looking at him/her, nodding, taking notes if necessary. When you do respond, acknowledge the emotion you have heard. For example: "Mrs. Jones, you sound upset about the photocopy policy." Or "It is frustrating to have to wait in line." Note that by validating the emotion, by showing sympathy, we do not necessarily agree with the person's point of view or approve of the accompanying behavior (e.g., yelling or pounding the desk). Acknowledging high emotion is often the most potent method of defusing it simply because it is unexpected. And strong emotions which are not recognized act as static during the discussion. Remember to listen and to acknowledge the emotion before moving to solutions.

### Don't Explain

After listening, avoid the impulse to explain. Only offer explanations if the patron specifically asks for them. Explanations appear defensive. Do not justify as that looks like a deflection of responsibility. The patron wants you to take responsibility for solving the problem, no matter what the cause.

If the library has inadvertently caused the anger, this is the right moment to apologize. Even if the library is not at fault, an apology "for the inconvenience" of "for having caused such trouble" can make an irate person feel better. Apologizing, of course, does not necessarily mean outright acceptance of blame; it simply means that you are sorry for the patron's discomfort. For example: "I'm sorry about the delay. Now I can help you." Or: "I am sorry that you are upset. What can we do to help the situation?"

In the case of a patron making unfounded accusations about the library or staff (you!), do not respond reflexively.[4] Do not repeat the negative buzzword or accusatory label or the conversation will sound like this to onlookers: "If this library wasn't so backwards . . ." "Backwards? Who are you calling backwards? We're not backwards! It's just that . . ." Note that the word "backwards" has now been put into context with the library four times. Even if sorely tempted, do not discuss the accusation itself. Instead, acknowledge the emotion and then move to a discussion of the patron's problem or need. If the accusation catches you off guard, simply bargain for a moment to collect your thoughts. For example:

"I never expected to hear anything like that. Let me think about it for a minute so that I can figure out a way to help you."

### Identify the Need

Next restate the problem clearly and concisely. It is important to restate the problem, not the solution offered by the patron. For example, a patron may demand that a reference book be loaned overnight against library policy. That is a possible solution to a different problem — that the patron needs some information found in the book. By separating needs from solutions we are able to identify many more alternatives. For example: "You weren't allowed to check out the book you wanted (restatement of problem). I can see that that would be upsetting (validation). It's a shame this book does not leave the library, but we have some others on the same topic which can be checked out . . ." It's clear that solutions would not have been discussed and the patron would have left the library disgruntled if the staff person had responded simply "No, that book cannot be checked out. It's library policy . . ."

If the patron's concern covers many issues, deal with them one at a time. For example: "It sounds as if we have a number of things to talk about. Let's take them one at a time, starting with your expired borrowing card . . ." Whenever possible, start with a problem which is easily solved or an error which can easily be conceded. This makes the library (and you) appear to be responsive and flexible and encourages the patron to act accordingly.

### Action

The more alternative solutions available, the better. It is important to let the patron choose among the possibilities to ensure that the solution is acceptable. Always explain what action will be taken and check that the patron understands. For example: "You have a few options. If you have identification with you, we can issue you a temporary card allowing you to check this out for two days. Or you can photocopy the chapter you need at ten cents a page. Of course, if you fill out this application today you can come back next week when your new library card is ready and check the book out for the full two weeks."

If the upset person cannot be mollified by any of these techniques, perhaps another staff member should take over. Although many libraries require their employees to call a supervisor in times of stress, actually any other calm person can do the trick. It is essential not to mislead the patron into thinking that the next employee is the one with all the power you lack, the one who will give in. Instead try something without unnecessary promises: "I can't seem to help you with this. Let me get someone who may be able to." Not only are two heads better than one at problem solving, but the time it takes to get another staff person allows the patron additional cooling off time and allows the upset employee a graceful exit.

Another technique is to take the patron to a different area in the library. Again, this allows for a cooling off period. More importantly, this removes the soap box for a patron who may be enjoying the attention s/he is receiving from other library users. Rather than making it seem like a punishment, suggest that moving elsewhere will be beneficial. For example: "I would like to hear more about this, but not here. Why don't we move into another room where we can sit down." Or: "This is important. I think we can discuss it better in the office."

Sometimes there are no solutions which fit library policy and will please the patron. It is still possible to minimize the person's anger—and the negative reaction to the library—by stating that you will take action. For example, even promising to write a memo to the library director about the issue, offering to voice it at a staff meeting, or recommending that the patron use the suggestion box are better than flatly stating that "there's nothing we can do."

### More Serious Confrontations

If the patron moves beyond acceptable expressions of anger, it is essential that the staff person speak and act assertively. Assertiveness requires the speaker to use "I statements" rather than "You statements," minimizing blame and defensiveness. This is done with a three part statement.[5] First, offer a sympathetic statement which validates the emotion. Then label the problem behavior and state the result of that behavior. Be careful to label the behavior—not the person—and to state the result with as little accusation as possible. Last, suggest a method for dealing with the behavior. All of these components should be integrated into one short speech, allowing for no patron comments until you are done. For example: "I can understand that you are upset (validation). Yelling (problem behavior) upsets me so that I am unable to think clearly about good solutions (result). Why don't we move away from the desk and discuss this quietly over here (method)."

If the patron shows overt aggression which threatens staff, other patrons, or library property and the above approach is ineffective, repeat the policy or rule in question and calmly offer the patron one last alternative. "Throwing books is not allowed in the library. You must either calm down or leave the library." If the patron's conduct does not improve, follow your library's written policies for illegal behaviors.

## OUR OWN ANGER

Studies have shown that only 10% of people who are yelled at handle it well. Twenty percent become furious, scream back, and retain an angry frustration. The rest — 70% — act defensive or frightened, feeling paralyzed or upset.[6] We all need to find methods for coping with the emotions that arise from being yelled at by an angry patron.

### To Do Right After the Angry Encounter

First, don't forget to breathe. When angry or anxious, many people tend to hold their breath. But we need the fresh oxygen which breathing pumps into our blood cells and body tissues. The most calming breathing is done with a deep inhale through the nose and a slow exhale through the mouth. Because our physical and emotional responses are so interconnected, by relaxing the body we can calm the mind. Composing our breathing and placing our body in a relaxed, open posture can help to soothe us. Doing yoga or transcendental meditation also work on both the body and mind; both of these techniques take study and practice. I find that a simple progressive muscle relaxation exercise can be invaluable — and can be done inconspicuously anywhere, including behind the reference desk. In this technique, each group of muscles is first tightened and then slowly relaxed. For example, the hands are clenched into a tight fist for a count of five and then slowly opened over a count of five. Neck, shoulder, arm, knee, ankle, and toes are each done. Afterwards, the muscles feel warm and loose as the blood flows back into them.[7] Next, accept that you are angry, that everyone gets angry, that anger is okay. But how we feel and what we do with the feelings are separate issues. Having a feeling doesn't necessarily mean acting on it.[8] In other words, anger doesn't have to result in yelling at someone. After all, don't you wish that patron had realized this?

### Longer Term Approaches

Library employees who work with the public are bound to find themselves coping with angry patrons — and then their own resultant anger and stress. To prepare ourselves, we need to analyze our own and others' patterns of anger management. To do this, we have to observe our own characteristic styles of managing anger, note the sequences which tend to anger us, and observe how others manage their anger.[9]

While observing our own situational reactions, we also need to consider thinking patterns which may make us angry. There are many irrational thought patterns which make people defensive or antagonistic. For example, everyone has "red flag" words which "push our buttons." Maybe the word "librarian" or "censorship" or the name of a certain political party is enough to make us defensive. Labels and stereotypes cause people to think and act irrationally, as do generalizations which are powerful emotionally but weak in logic. We need to be aware of the words and generalizations that cause us to feel, or to hold onto, anger.

Here is one six-step model of irrational decisions leading to anger:[10]

- I want something. (e.g., to be treated with respect)
- I didn't get it and I'm frustrated. (That patron was rude to me)
- It is awful and terrible not to get what I want.

- I shouldn't be frustrated.
- You (read: the patron) are bad for frustrating me.
- Bad people ought to be punished.

Though most of us would hate to admit that we ever sink into such childish, specious reasoning, this method of magnification and self-frustration is common.

Finally, we need to recognize that our anger is a secondary emotion—just as we know that the patron's is—and to ask ourselves what the underlying emotions and real issues are. Depending on the answers, the question of responsibility emerges: Who is responsible for those feelings of embarrassment, ineptitude, loss of esteem, frustration? What am I willing to do about those parts which are my personal responsibility, e.g., defensive attitudes, difficulty working with the public, personal problems with stress management? And who can I turn to for assistance with the items which are the library's responsibility, e.g., understaffing, inadequate training, unenforcable policies, procedural difficulties?

## INSTITUTIONAL RESPONSES

This brings us to a discussion of what the library administration can do to assist its employees with both the difficulty of defusing angry patrons and the problems of "anger fallout." The first such tool of the administration is the library's policies. Most libraries have written policies about problem behavior in the library, but few of these address the angry patron. Even fewer include provisions for helping the employee involved.

### A Matter of Policy

A good library policy should distinguish between acceptable and non-acceptable angry behavior by patrons. It should state the consequences of unacceptable behavior and outline the procedures staff should use in those situations. It should also stipulate that any library employee who deals with angry patrons is entitled to support from the administration. This support can take many forms.

For example, some libraries follow procedures which require the employee to call a supervisor when dealing with a difficult confrontation—yet the supervisor is rarely present. The policy should be rewritten to allow any other employee to come to the aid of a staff member with an irate patron. After the confrontation itself, libraries can offer support. Some libraries have regularly scheduled "blow out" sessions at which staff can ventilate their frustrations. Others have a "buddy system" wherein each public service employee is assigned another staff member with whom to share any difficult problems. Some libraries require written incident reports, even when the patron's behavior has been officially acceptable; such reports encourage the staff person to "get it out," keep the administration informed as to the kinds of stresses its employees deal with on a daily basis, and allow patterns of difficult behavior from any one patron to be documented.

### The Law of Requisite Variety

In cybernetics, the law of requisite variety states that the element with the highest range of variability is the one that will control the machine. This can be restated as "whoever has the most options has the best odds of getting what s/he wants." If libraries want to satisfy their patrons, they need to supply their staff with many alternatives to increase the chances that they will have what the patron needs. Certainly libraries do this in terms of multiple formats of materials, varied hours of operation, and differing types of services. But library procedures need to have a built-in flexibility as well so that the reference librarian can minimize the use of "I am sorry, but I can't do that; it's against library policy." Library staff can be ingenious at thinking up alternative solutions, but only if the administration allows these options. Reference and circulation staff should brainstorm possible solutions to familiar patron problems and administrators should consider them for approval. In the private sector, salespeople are given "rebuttal files." These are rejoinders to customers' common excuses not to buy the proffered item. Telephone salespeople always use them. For instance, an appliance store calls to offer refrigerators on sale. When the potential customer responds that s/he already has a refrigerator, the sales representative does not hang up. Rather s/he has a ready response from the rebuttal file. I recommend that libraries develop such lists for their staff. What are the most common concerns of your patrons — the questions whose answers you know will upset them? Staff should collaborate on possible responses which may be less upsetting. For example, if your new security system frustrates many patrons per day, what could staff say to placate them? Having a list of rejoinders is especially helpful to the staff member whose mind goes blank when confronted by an irate library user.

### Alternatives for the Patron Too

The patron, too, needs alternative methods for coping with anger. One simple old-fashioned approach is to provide a complaint (or suggestion) box which encourages patrons to share their concerns in writing to the administration rather than in person to the desk staff. Another is to invite letters directly to the library director when patrons are dissatisfied. Again, this is a good topic for brainstorming by the staff who know the patrons best.

## WHY BOTHER?

Consumer research shows that 90% of discontent customers never return — and tell 9 of their friends about their unhappiness. Moreover, the unhappy customer remembers his/her problem for 23.5 months whereas the satisfied customer remembers for eighteen months.[11] Now that libraries are becoming more aware of their need for public relations, our ability to satisfy even our difficult patrons is essential. Of course, the library's services, collections, and facilities are paramount to patron satisfaction. But the way we deal with each dissatisfied library user one-on-one can compensate for lacks in the other areas. And recent research found that patrons were the major source of stress to library staff. However, they were also the most commonly cited source of satisfaction for library workers.[12] If we can reduce the stressful encounters with patrons and multiply the satisfying ones, life at the reference desk will be more enjoyable for all.

# REFERENCES

1. Stearns, Carol Z. and Peter N. Stearns. *Anger: The Struggle for Emotional Control in America's History*. Chicago: University of Chicago Press, 1986.
2. Gaylin, Willard. *The Rage Within: Anger in Modern Life*. NY: Simon & Schuster, 1984.
3. *Ibid.*
4. Lustberg, Arch. *Winning When It Really Counts*. NY: Simon & Schuster, 1988. p. 89-109.
5. Bolton, Robert. *People Skills*. NY: Simon & Schuster, 1979.
6. Bramson, Robert. *Coping With Difficult People . . . In Business and in Life*. NY: Ballantine, 1981.
7. For more on relaxation techniques, see Benson, Herbert M. *The Relaxation Response*. NY: Avon, 1976 and Weisinger, Hendrie. *Dr. Weisinger's Anger Workout Book*. NY: Quill, 1985.
8. Black, Claudia. *Repeat After Me*. Denver: MAC Publishing, 1987. p.26.
9. Lerner, Harriet Goldhor. *The Dance of Anger*. NY: Simon & Schuster, 1985. P. 190-194.
10. Hauck, Paul A. *Overcoming Frustration and Anger*. Philadelphia: Westminster Press, 1974. Based on the work of Albert Ellis.
11. Research done for the White House Office on Consumer Affairs, discussed in Desatnick, R. L. *Managing to Keep the Customer*. San Francisco: Jossey Bass, 1987.
12. Bunge, Charles. "Stress in the Library." *Library Journal* 112 (15): 47-51, September, 15, 1987.

# BIBLIOGRAPHY

Bolton, Robert. *People Skills: How to Assert Yourself, Listen to Others, and Resolve Conflict*. NY: Simon & Schuster, 1979.
Bramson, Robert M. *Coping With Difficult People . . . In Business and in Life*. NY: Ballantine, 1981.
Conroy, Barbara and Barbara Schindler Jones. *Improving Communication in the Library*. Phoenix, AZ: Oryx Press, 1986.
Drescher, Jeanne P. *The Hitting Habit: Anger Control for Battering Couples*. NY: MacMillan, 1984.
Ellis, Albert. *Anger: How to Live With and Without It*. Secaucus, NJ: Citadel Press, 1977.
Elgin, Suzanne Haden. *The Gentle Art of Verbal Self-Defense*. NY: Prentice Hall, 1980 and *The Gentle Art of Verbal Self-Defense Workbook*. NY: Dorset Press, 1987.
Folger, J. and M. Poole. *Working Through Conflict: A Communication Perspective*. NY: Scott, Foresman, and Co., 1984.

Gaylin, Willard. *The Rage Within: Anger in Modern Life*. NY: Simon & Schuster, 1984.

Hauck, Paul A. *Overcoming Frustration and Anger*. Philadelphia: Westminster Press, 1974.

Lerner, Harriet Goldhor. *The Dance of Anger*. NY: Harper, 1985.

Lustberg, Arch. *Winning When It Really Counts*. NY: Simon & Schuster, 1988.

Matthews, Anne J. *Communicate: A Librarian's Guide to Interpersonal Communications*. Chicago: ALA, 1983.

Stearns, Carol Z. and Peter N. Stearns. *Anger: The Struggle for Emotional Control in America's History*. Chicago: University of Chicago Press, 1986.

Tavris, Carol. "Anger Defused." *Psychology Today* 16(11): 25-34, November 1982.

Tavris, Carol. *Anger: The Misunderstood Emotion*. NY: Simon & Schuster, 1982.

Weisinger, Hendrie. *Dr. Weisinger's Anger Workout Book*. NY: Quill Press, 1985.

Wells, T. Keeping Your Cool Under Fire. NY: McGraw-Hill, 1980.

# II. SPECIAL POPULATIONS IN THE LIBRARY

# "No One Wants To See Them": Meeting the Reference Needs of the Deinstitutionalized

## Fay Zipkowitz

**SUMMARY.** With the continuing trend of deinstitutionalizing persons with physical, mental, and emotional disabilities, and the development of community based housing and social services to these populations, libraries are now acquiring potential users with special needs which many libraries and their collective staffs are ill prepared to serve. This article describes these populations, examines some of the information needs, and presents methods of providing service and a rationale for community outreach. The state program in Rhode Island is outlined, describing efforts to reach community residents through their public libraries and the state operated Bookmobile.

Fay Zipkowitz is Associate Professor at the Graduate School of Library and Information Studies, University of Rhode Island, Kingston, RI. From January 1981 through August 1986 she was Director, Rhode Island Department of State Library Services. The author acknowledges Andrew Egan, Frank Iacono and Ann L. Piascik at DSLS, for their thoughtful assistance and for sharing their experiences for this article and extends special thanks also to Patricia Del Nero, graduate assistant, GSLIS.

Note to the reader: The following statement is a paraphrase of the response to a question I asked of a state library staff member (not Rhode Island) about services to the deinstitutionalized. The response came in one long burst and was disturbing and stimulating at the same time. I have used it as the point of departure to ask, and seek answers to, some questions about the impact of a new category of special populations on library reference services and staff.

"No one wants to see them. They are terrible to look at. They're depressing. I suppose we are going to have to do something about these people but so far I've avoided it. I mean, who wants to deal with them? Who even wants to even see them? They are terrible to look at. All crippled up, some of them. Can't talk or wipe their own chins. And then there are the retards and the mentals. They look funny and act funny. Terrible. Depressing. Don't look so shocked. A lot of people feel the way I do but won't admit to it. Why, there's a group home that opened up near my apartment building and I have to walk past it on my way to the bus stop. Every day they've got these people out on the street where they are right in plain sight. Some even ride the bus, who knows where. Turns my stomach to look at them. There ought to be a limit to what we librarians are asked to do to serve people. They don't need books and stuff anyway. Maybe a movie once in a while to keep them quiet. And you see them everywhere — restaurants, supermarkets, everywhere. Terrible. They're hopeless and depressing. No one wants to see them. They should be put back where they came from, out of sight. I don't know what we can do for them. When I first started out we weren't expected to deal with these people. We're librarians, for heaven's sake. We should serve the people who can get something out of reading and so forth. I don't want to look at them. No one wants to see them."

Such a statement from a professional charged with serving under-served or unserved populations gets one thinking. Is this librarian right? Are people who have been out of the mainstream of public library service not serveable? Are their information needs trivial, non-existent or beyond our competence? Is it only an attitude problem on our part as librarians, or are new approaches and definitions of reference responses needed for a new service sector? In this article I will attempt to look at who the deinstitutionalized are, what some of their reference and information needs are, and some approaches to meeting these needs.

## WHO THEY ARE

Disabilities take many forms within the three broad categories of physically, mentally, and emotionally disabled. There are differences in kind and degree of disability, and many people may be disabled in more than one capacity. In recent times disabled people were not in plain sight. Because of their special needs, and the fears and frustrations of the able bodied, the disabled were kept hidden at home, as invalids, or institutionalized, where they may have received custodial care or minimal education or rehabilitation. The movement toward integrating disabled people into the community, or deinstitutionalization, took hold in the 1980's. Not the least of the reasons was the growing mental health movement, which deemed the warehouse approach to be obsolete and inhumane, costly in both human and financial resources. A series of court cases were decided in favor of patients' rights, including issues of involuntary treatment and incarceration. Non-standard behavior caused by certain disabilities can now be controlled by psychoactive drugs, enabling more people to live outside of institutional settings.[1]

The growing demands of physically disabled people for physical access to buildings, transportation, education and gainful employment have also contributed to the gradual modification of existing facilities and programs, and the stricter requirements for unimpeded access to new buildings, educational and training programs, and public events in the community. A logical sequel to these trends is community based residences and workshops which can provide much more personalized and normalized settings than institutions, and can provide opportunities otherwise available to the general public.

The disabled populations now moving into the community include the mentally retarded, the mentally ill, the developmentally disabled, and the physically disabled. They make up an estimated population of about 36 million people, or 16% of the U. S. population. Of these, approximately 11 million are gainfully employed, and another 15 million could work if given the opportunities to do so.[2] Some are born with disabilities, but about five out of six will develop disabilities later in life.[3] In their book *Library and Information Services for Handicapped Individuals,* Wright and Davie review in some detail legal and legislated definitions of disabled people.[4]

People in group homes or independent living programs frequently have been removed from large, highly structured, isolated institutional settings. They may be severely disabled people who need an attendant or skilled nursing care on a permanent basis or they may be individuals moving toward independent living who are using the group facility to receive support and counseling while in transition. A third category includes people who prefer to, or who are advised to, remain in a sheltered environment while still participating in noninstitutional activities.[5] For the purposes of this article they have two things in common: first, they are people who have been, or would be in other times, out of sight and locked up for most or all of their lives; second, they are people we as librarians are not accustomed to dealing with. In all other ways they are individuals with distinct personalities and requirements. They may be friendly or mistrustful; patient or impatient; angry or good humored; likeable or irritating; perceptive or insensitive; self aware or oblivious; arrogant or humble; socialized or awkward; verbal or silent. Rehabilitation experts estimate that almost 3/4 of our population will eventually experience some disability.[6] The disabled are very much like to rest of us, although they may need special response based on their individual disabilities.

### WHERE ARE THEY?

Statistics on deinstitutionalized populations are difficult to track down. Most programs are state based and administered, and sources such as the *American Statistics Index* and the *Reference Statistics Index* do not include the heading "Deinstitutionalized." When these sources do have listings for community based facilities, they refer to correctional programs. Numbers can be found in some sources by particular category of disability, usually from advocate or service organizations. By definition a certain portion of the deinstitutionalized will remain uncounted because they are not living in group facilities or participating in community based services.

The best sources of information about people who have been moved into the local community relate to the state and local level. Most alternate care facilities are run or monitored by state and county agencies. Agencies which fund and/or supervise facilities for the mentally impaired, the retarded, the training of disabled people for employment, etc., can provide directories of facilities in the community, and the names of directors or caregivers. From that point on, the library should become involved in a familiar activity: the community needs assessment. In order to know what the reference or information needs of a population are, the staff will have to find out about the local residents, their activities, their goals, and the kinds of library services they will need. A number of library publications have suggestions for serving special populations, usually organized by type of disability, and some references are provided at the end of this article.

## *WHAT DO THEY NEED?*

Since deinstitutionalized people are trying to integrate themselves into the outside world, some of their information needs focus on life skills. They may be seeking information on the availability of job counseling and training. Personal health skills and self care, money management skills, home management, consumer information, and community mobility are also areas of individual learning for independent living. Velleman outlines information needs and gives suggestions of printed and audio/visual sources to respond to them.[7] One of the areas she covers is the need for information on benefits and entitlements under the law. People with physical disabilities may need information on adaptive clothing, housing and employment. Travel and transportation, recreational and leisure activities, the arts, alternative communications media, and accessible programming are also included in Velleman's list. Personal development and sexuality may be awkward topics for librarians to grapple with, but they are topics of concern to many disabled people and among the most important to some as they go through a socializing process for the first time in their lives. The reference needs of the developmentally disabled follow a similar pattern, as outlined by Cagle.[8] He refers to social, personal, economic and other normalized living skills as areas of information sought by people who are moving from institutional (and sometimes dehumanized) settings. Allegri describes reference interaction with physically disabled people, with suggestions for enhancing communication and providing needed assistance without being condescending.[9] Respect for the privacy and dignity of deinstitutionalized patrons must be on the same level as for other library patrons.

Librarians are being called on to serve not only the deinstitutionalized persons themselves, but also their parents, teachers, caregivers, physicians, and other professionals working in the community facilities or in the supervising or contracting public agencies. The role of these people may be as intermediary or interpreter of information to aid the disabled, or they may in fact be the information seekers. They are in either case key sources for the library's analysis of how to serve the new community populations. Cagle reminds us that the relationship between the caregivers or supervisors or case managers and the reference librarian is crucial, and can make the difference between the client reaching independence or remaining dependent.[10] He also states that the reference librarian can "serve as a link between a wide variety of retrieval sources including tailored computer information services . . . By accessing reference services the case manager can receive more comprehensive and quality information on a particular subject than he could by conducting a sporadic random search through limited, outdated information sources."[11]

Disabled people may need physical assistance from their caregivers or companions in order to physically use the library at all, and if special arrangements or appointments are necessary they should be set up in advance.[12] The determination of such needs could emerge from the community assessment and discussion with the care providers or supervisors, and can become part of the library's planning or programming for the special populations.

Allegri discusses assumptions, mistakes, misconceptions and possible solutions to the problems they create in reference transactions with disabled people. Stereotypical thinking and emotional reactions have to be overcome before good communication can take place. She suggests some general guidelines which can be helpful with the new library information seekers:

1. Be aware of body language or nonverbal cues, especially with communication disorders;
2. Focus on the person, not the disability;
3. Approach the patron with respect, acceptance, and warmth as opposed to disapproval or reserve;
4. Avoid pity;
5. Offer assistance as one would to any other patron displaying some difficulty using the library;
6. Know the library's collection and services in terms of special needs of disabled patrons;
7. Design services, where necessary, to accommodate special needs.[13]

Knowing something about the specific disabilities of patrons, and their manifestations and symptoms, can help librarians tailor their responses in the most appropriate fashion. A pamphlet entitled *Handicapping Characteristics* published by Very Special Arts of Indiana describes various disabilities and gives suggestions for working with individuals, with specific approaches for each disability.[14] Van Hoven describes specially designed staff training programs for librarians in public libraries as part of an LSCA funded program in southern California.[15]

Allegri also highlights some of the library services already available which may be of particular use to the deinstitutionalized disabled and their companions — telephone reference services, online bibliographic databases, photocopying and audiovisual services.[16] To this might be added interlibrary loan, document delivery, aid in selecting or synthesizing materials at the appropriate level, and referral to appropriate public service agencies and their data banks.

Keeping in mind the considerable differences in deinstitutionalized individuals, the community analysis by the local library is likely to be the best first step in assessing and meeting the information needs of the new neighbors. Velleman reminds us to avoid the "spread" effect: the concept that if a person has one disability he or she is totally incapacitated in all mental and physical areas; and she cautions us to view disabled people without unrealistic expectations of courageousness, humility, gratitude or acceptance on their part.[17] Several sources suggest methods of reference interaction based on type of service rather than type of disability, and also make suggestions for interaction with inchoate patrons based on principles of human learning psychology and "a helping system which will facilitate that learning."[18]

There is one major category of deinstitutionalized person which may be the most difficult for libraries to serve — those who are on their own in the community without adequate support systems or with poor preparation for independent living, and those who are homeless and likewise without social and educational support. According to an analysis prepared by the U.S. Department of Health and Human Services of local studies conducted in several major metropolitan areas, between 25% and 40% of the homeless single adults are mentally disabled.[19] When reference services are used by individuals without adequate social support, the library's response must be on an individual basis. There is no mediator or interpreter in the form of a caseworker or caregiver, nor is there any preparation of staff such as might be gained from outreach to group facilities and from becoming familiar with particular disabilities. The library is faced with what is called, for want of better terminology, the "problem patron." Salter and Salter document the results of "emancipation from treatment and support" as being homelessness and problematic behavior for public agencies such as libraries, and recommend some methods and actions for coping.[20]

Without the mediation or companion both the expression of information needs and the ability to interpret the information response are very complicated and will require time and effort the library may find difficult to provide. Is this a segment of the population we will never be able to adequately provide with reference services? The statement at the beginning of this article begins to haunt one when considering the "free," unsupported, or non-affiliated deinstitutionalized individual.

## RESPONSE ON THE LOCAL LEVEL

This section describes the efforts of state agencies and local libraries in Rhode Island to provide reference services to the deinstitutionalized populations.

Since 1980 the numbers of individuals who reside in state institutions has steadily declined. As of 1988, the Rhode Island Department of Mental Health, retardation and Hospitals estimates that 5,300 individuals are receiving mental health services at the community support level, and about 1,000 individuals with developmental disabilities are living in group homes, semi-independent apartments or family arrangements. The state is committed to closing the state residence for persons with mental retardation and developmental disabilities by July 1991. In December 1987, only 223 residents remained at the facility. In March of 1989, 195 remained. Other state facilities show similar dramatic decline in resident populations.[21]

The Rhode Island Department of State Library Services has taken a two pronged approach to helping the deinstitutionalized become integrated into their local library community and to become rational users of the information available in libraries. Two Institutional Consultants have been working with special populations and their caregivers, and have been involved with helping local libraries respond to their new users. For more than three years, the Department's Bookmobile has included stops at ten sheltered workshops for adults with mental retardation. Ann Piascik, Institutional Consultant, initiated and continues this service. The Bookmobile's primary focus since 1981 has been on isolated populations — senior citizen housing, nursing homes and community centers. In bringing the Bookmobile to the sheltered workshops, the intent was not to replace or supplement public library service (as in the case of the isolated populations) but rather to provide a transitional experience for users to become familiar with, and to become comfortable with, what most of us consider to be traditional, normal library interactions. One workshop has already been able to terminate Bookmobile service and use the local public library, and another is preparing to do likewise in June of 1989.

The Bookmobile has served as a training library enabling the

users to become familiar with library rules and procedures as well
as to develop responsibility for borrowed materials and to learn to
make reasoned choices. At the same time, Bookmobile service can
concentrate on targeted collections of interest to these new users,
and on teaching the socialization skills necessary to use a public
library. With increasing mobility, the workshop and group homes
have been able to expand their options and take advantage of the
wider array of materials and services at the public libraries. Since
about half of all public libraries in Rhode Island are part of an online borrowing system, which includes DSLS, many Bookmobile
users and local public library patrons are able to utilize the resources of the state very efficiently. They have learned to use the
readers' advisors and the reserve function which are available to
public library patrons, and to approach the reference transaction
with some degree of confidence. The DSLS Institutional Consultants distribute directories of community based programs to public
libraries and are available to consult with local libraries on the development of plans and appropriate services to alternate care facility
residents. They also gave each public library a copy of *New Life in
the Neighborhood* by Robert Perske (see listing of Additional
Sources). Having worked with special populations in both the institutional and local settings, the consultants are able to assist local
public librarians in assessing and meeting the information needs of
their new users. Andrew Egan, Institutional Consultant, summarizes his experience and provides advice based on working with
local libraries as follows:

> Libraries have made their buildings accessible to physically
> disabled individuals with curb cuts, ramps and interior access
> points — rest rooms, elevators and drinking fountains. To go
> beyond this, librarians need to address the needs of the special
> populations entering their community. Initially this will mean
> developing an outreach program to make new residents aware
> of the services of the library. The Reference Librarian should
> know where the group homes, apartment complexes, commu-
> nity centers and alternate care facilities are located in their
> community. The public relations efforts should concentrate on

these facilities in order to let the new members of the community know they are welcomed.

At the same time, the Reference Librarian can gather information about services to special populations and identify what services the library can offer immediately and in the future. In service training sessions which inform all staff about the special populations can be developed with assistance from the Reference Librarian. It is important for each member of the staff to be aware of the differences among people who may be physically disabled, mentally ill, mentally retarded, or have some other developmental disability.

In terms of collecting resources useful to the new populations being served, the Reference Librarian will need information about daily living skills, job and career interests and training, community agency information and information relating to recreational activities. The print resources need to accommodate differing levels of reading ability, and the text should be set in a typeface which is easily visible. Formats for non-print materials should cover a variety of appropriate media, and include materials for individual as well as group use or viewing.

The Reference Librarian should also look at computer resources which the general public has access to in the library. Adaptive devices which make the computer useable by a person with a disability may need to be purchased, such as an "adaptive firmware card" with a variety of options which make the computer accessible to a person who has a physical or mental disability. The Reference Librarian will need to receive training in this area, and should also seek the advice of other professionals who work in related areas—physical therapists, adaptive device technicians, and computer experts, to name a few.

## CONCLUSION

"More troubling than the struggle against governmental or institutional neglect is that against the deep rooted and pervasive antipathy toward the handicapped. 'This is the ultimate barrier for the disabled and the most difficult to clear away,' says Douglas A. Fenderson, director of the National Institute of Handicapped research."[22]

In recent years the focus on rehabilitative medicine and engineering for the disabled has led to the development of remarkable new devices, including applications in robotics and computers, improved telecommunication devices and other aids such as speech synthesizers.

The movement to permit disabled people to be as independent and socially productive as their abilities allow will force community agencies to respond in ways that previously were not thought appropriate. No one can function at his or her potential in the modern world without access to information resources, least of all those populations which have been disadvantaged physically, mentally or emotionally. Libraries are among the last bastions of democracy in public services, and as the ranks of the deinstitutionalized and never institutionalized grow, the library has a powerful role to play in their successful integration into the complex social world in which we all live. These populations are neither static not homogeneous, but rather are a dynamic and ever changing clientele with individual needs and levels of potential achievement.

Before concluding with a response to the statement which begins this article, a review of assumptions may be helpful.

1. Libraries are hard to use; that is why reference librarians need education, training, experience and strong interpersonal skills.
2. Just as with the population at large, not every deinstitutionalized person or caregiver perceives the need for the informational resources of the library.
3. We are encountering a population unfamiliar with libraries and the overwhelming array of informational resources, research methodologies and strategies, and user services (not to mention all the traditions, conventions and fetishes that only librarians understand). Some orientation for both staff and users is in order to span this cultural gulf.
4. Reference service to the deinstitutionalized must be appropriate to their needs and goals, and special reference skills may be required to meet those needs and goals.

5. Mediation and interpretive support are helpful in reference transactions when they clarify the question or when they inform the staff.
6. In keeping with the library's service ethic, the right of privacy, and dignity and respect of all users must be maintained.

My conclusion in response to the maker of the opening statement: you had better be wrong! Reference librarians have adapted to new technologies, changing mores and standards of behavior, and are already responding to and adapting to the special needs of these newly visible users.

## REFERENCES

1. Charles A. Salter and Jeffrey L. Salter. *On the Front Lines: Coping with the Library's Problem Patrons*. Englewood, CO: Libraries Unlimited, 1988. p. xxi.
2. Bonnie Milstein. (American Association on Mental Deficiency). U.S. House. Committee on Education and Labor. "The Parental and Medical Leave Act of 1986." Hearing, Apr. 22, 1986. Washington, DC: GPO, 1986. p. 44.
3. Laurence Cherry and Rona Cherry. "New Hope For The Disabled." *The New York Times Magazine*, Feb. 5, 1984. p. 52.
4. Kieth C. Wright and Janice F. Davie. *Library and Information Services for Handicapped Individuals*. 2nd Ed. Littleton, CO: Libraries Unlimited, 1983.
5. Ruth A. Velleman. *Serving Physically Disabled People: An Information Handbook For All Libraries*. New York: R.R. Bowker, 1979. p. 3.
6. Cherry and Cherry, p. 52.
7. Velleman, Chapter 8 (pp. 162-70).
8. R. Brantley Cagle, Jr. "Reference Service to the Developmentally Disabled: Normalization of Access." *Catholic Library World*. 54/8:266-70. February 1983 p. 269.
9. Francesca Allegri. "On The Other Side of the Reference Desk: The Patron with a Physical Disability." *Medical Reference Services Quarterly* 3(3) Fall 1984:65-76.
10. Cagle, p. 270.
11. Cagle, p. 270.
12. Allegri, p. 74.
13. Allegri, p. 68.
14. *Handicapping Characteristics: A Guide for the Arts Community*. Indianapolis, IN: Very Special Arts of Indiana.
15. James Van Hoven. "Involving Developmentally Disabled Adults in Public Library Service." In *Library Services to Developmentally Disabled Children*

*and Adults*. Ed. by Linda Lucas. Chicago: Association of Specialized and Cooperative Library Agencies, (ASCLA Occasional Paper, no.1) 1982.

    16. Allegri, p. 73.

    17. Velleman, p. 5-6.

    18. See, for example, *The Mainstreamed Library*. ed. by Baskins and Harris; *The Library as a Learning Service Center*, by Penland and Matheu; *Library Services to Developmentally Disabled Children and Adults*, ed. by Linda Lucas; and, *Improving Library Service to Physically Disabled Persons: A Self-Evaluation Checklist* by Needham and Jahoda.

    19. U.S. House. Committee on Appropriations. Department of Housing and Urban Development . . . Appropriations for 1987. Washington, DC: GPO, 1986. p. 304-5.

    20. Salter, p. xxi.

    21. Rhode Island Department of Mental Health, Retardation and Hospitals. *1988 Status Report*. Cranston, RI: MHRH, 1988; and *Open Lines*, published quarterly by the Division of Retardation and Developmental Disabilities, Rhode Island Department of Mental Health, Retardation and Hospitals. March 1989.

    22. Cherry and Cherry, p. 60.

## ADDITIONAL SOURCES

*ALA Yearbook of Library and Information Services*. (Annual).

Jean M. Clarke. "Users with Special Needs." *In British Librarianship and Information Work*, 1981-85, v.1. London: Library Association, 1988.pp.168-85.

Meliza Jackson. "Mental Health Information? Yes, But Not in My Neighborhood." *Catholic Library World* 56:287-90 February 1985.

Debra Wilcox Johnson and Marcia Dennison Rossiter. "Planning Library Services for Special Needs Populations." *Public Libraries* 25:94-8 Fall 1986.

Kathleen Joyce Kruger. "Library Service to Disabled Citizens: Guidelines to Sources and Issues." *Technicalities* 4:8-9 September 1984.

*Library Services to Developmentally Disabled Children and Adults*. Ed. by Linda Lucas. Chicago, Association of Specialized and Cooperative Library Agencies, 1982.

Eunice Lovejoy. "Coping with Patrons Perceived as Problems: The Disabled Library Patron." *Ohio Library Association Bulletin* 56:27-8 April 1986.

*The Mainstreamed Library. Issues, Ideas, Innovations*. Ed. by Barbara H. Baskin and Karen H. Harris. Chicago: American Library Association, 1982.

Michael B. Murphy. "Library Services for the Disabled [In the Chicago Area]" *Catholic Library World* 59:172-5.

William L. Needham. *Improving Library Service to Physically Disabled Persons: A Self-Evaluation Checklist*. Littleton, CO: Libraries Unlimited, 1983.

Patric R. Penland and Aleyamma Mathai. *The Library As A Learning Service Center*. New York: M. Dekker, 1978.

Perske, Robert. *New Life in the Neighborhood. How Persons with Retardation or*

*Other Disabilities Can Help Make A Good Community Better*. Nashville: Abingdon, 1980.

*Populations of Residential Facilities for Persons with Mental Retardation: Trends by Size, Operation and State, 1977 to 1987*. Minneapolis, MN: Center for Residential and Community Services, Institute on Community Integration, University of Minnesota. (Brief Report #32) February, 1989.

# Serving the Older Adult

## Celia Hales-Mabry

**SUMMARY.** Services to older adults in libraries have historically been weak or absent. Research published as a result of the oft-cited Cleveland study of 1971 and 1973, an update by Betty Turock in 1984, and studies by Celia Hales-Mabry in 1980-81 and 1984, have supported this thesis. Guidelines published in 1987 by the American Library Association suggest a much-expanded role for libraries. If these guidelines are to become a reality, we must take steps to implement them by assertively enlisting the involvement of our peer librarians as well as the funding to support new services. Evaluated in detail are the four guidelines that most directly influence reference services to older adults.

"Serving the older adult" has been a concept given more credence in official documents of the American Library Association than in the day-to-day practice of our libraries. In 1987 the RASD Library Service to an Aging Population Committee of ALA sponsored "Guidelines for Library Service to Older Adults."[1] This document built upon several lengthy years of work and was a revision of guidelines published by ALA in 1975. Yet the famed "Cleveland study" of 1971 and 1973,[2] as well as an update to that study carried out in 1984 by Betty Turock[3] have conclusively demonstrated that library service to older adults has been and remains painfully inadequate. Moreover, my own studies among service providers to the aging and librarians (1980-81),[4] as well as the aging themselves (1984),[5] have found that only librarians perceive the library as an important means of satisfying informational need of the older adult. We have much to do.

Celia Hales-Mabry is Reference/Instruction Librarian in the O. Meredith Wilson Library, The University of Minnesota, 309 19th Avenue South, Minneapolis, MN 55455.

## THE GUIDELINES

The document published in 1987 merits careful study.[6] Based upon 12 proactive statements, it is laudable in its attempt to serve the needs of our elder clientele. Unfortunately, this document, like its predecessor, will remain a target for implementation rather than a *fait accompli* unless individuals working in libraries across the nation develop a greater interest in working with elders. Only a handful of individuals nation-wide in the last decade have been actively involved in the American Library Association's two forums for library service to the older adult (RASD's Library Service to an Aging Population and ASCLA's Library Service to the Impaired Elderly Forum). With the number of elderly increasing, we are missing the chance to make a major impact upon society if we fail to provide and to market the informational services that only a library can well provide.

The guidelines as a whole deserve study, but four of the statements are particularly important to the reference librarian; each of these will be discussed in turn.

*Guideline 1: Exhibit and promote a positive attitude toward the aging process and older adults.* It is sometimes difficult to keep a positive attitude about the older adult because of our own ambivalent attitudes about growing older. Growing older leads ultimately to death, a reality which, despite philosophical and/or religious beliefs, is not easy to handle or to accept. We have not yet come to terms with the aging process. And that attitude may spill over to the reference desk.

How many of us recognize that we treat the older adult differently at the reference desk? Does the fact that one may have to speak more loudly or assist in retrieving books make us respond almost on reflex and, in some sense, stereotypically? We have an obligation to treat our patrons as individuals, assisting more in some cases than in others, but never assuming that additional help is needed simply because the individual is older. In my own case, being in an academic library means that the older individual is likely to be a faculty member, and then we may indeed go the extra mile to ensure that needs are handled well and completely. In a public library, though, would I respond in that positive a manner? I should. I should not let any personal difficulties that I might have with growing older influence what happens with an older patron.

There is much concern at the grass roots about not "singling out" the elder. It is questionnable to what extent elders have this attitude vs. to what extent librarians believe that elders will be offended if targeted. Certainly the special "senior citizen" status is *enjoyed* by many in our society; special discounts are an obviously popular phenomenon. I would suggest that elders are less likely to be offended by special treatment than we think; growing old is not a disease.

*Guideline 2: Promote information and resources on aging and its implications not only to older adults themselves but also to family members, professionals in the field of aging, and other persons interested in the aging process.* We have a long way to go. The renowned Cleveland study, *National Survey of Library Services to the Aging,* published in 1971 and 1973, found that two-thirds of public libraries and state library agencies gave the aging the lowest program priority. Less than one percent of their budgets went to services to the aging. Funding was found to be the single greatest impediment to strengthened library services to the aging. The report estimated that less than two percent of the aging in the United States receive specific library service from public libraries.

Betty Turock's "Update" found that while there has been some limited progress in public library service for older adults over the past decade, there is little evidence that they are receiving the attention they warrant, attention in keeping with the growth in the size of the elder population and in the national interest in the aging. She notes that the results that she found are remarkably similar to the *National Survey*.

A study which I carried out in 1980-81 and published in 1982 queried gerontologists and other workers with the aging, as well as library/information professionals with recognized interest in working with the aging. Four questions drew specific attention to the services of the library as follows:

1. Library outreach programs through deposit materials (delivered to "senior citizen" centers, nutrition sites, etc.), book mobiles, books-by-mail, visits to the homebound and institutionalized.
2. Library workshops, programs, and forums for the aging with emphasis upon important issues affecting their lives.
3. Information and referral programs operated by public libraries.
4. Audiocassettes on topics of concern available through library reference department for phone listening. (All four ranked near the bottom in perceived importance as a means of meeting informational need of the aging.)

Librarians, however, not surprisingly, ranked the items relatively high.

A follow-up study carried out in 1984 among a random sample of 400 adults aged 65 and older found that the elders corroborated the thinking of the specialists in aging, e.g., the library was not perceived as an important place to visit. Betty Turock makes the point that elders' lack of interest in the library may be a reflection of the fare they have become accustomed to expect from the library. She also notes that these services, such as they are, have not been promoted.[7]

When you want to know something, do you think of going to the library? Probably yes, because we are librarians. But others do not. The answer? First, we may look to the elders themselves to satisfy their informational needs by actively marketing our services for this group. The best hope for us that the elders who have leisure time may turn to the library for programs to meet their needs, information and referral services, reference services, etc., in the times of the day that most of the rest of the population spend at work. But there are barriers. If there is no life-long habit of turning to the library, we will need to market aggressively our services. We have not done so in the past, largely citing lack of funding as the reason. If the funding were there, would we do it? If we can enthusiastically say "yes," then we must think of ways to energize our co-workers with the same zeal that we feel.

Second, we must reach out to younger people who have contact with elders. It is a myth that the children of the elderly fail to care for their parents' and grandparents' needs.[8] The fact that this myth is so pervasive in our society is particularly misfortunate, because it leads elders to wonder what the road ahead will bring. Reaching out to these caregivers, sometimes directly through information and referral services sponsored by the library, will do much to solidify the image of the library in our society.

Third, we must seek to engage our colleagues in gerontology with jointly-sponsored programs. Bessie Moore and Christina Young have documented that such cooperation is occurring at a greater rate than formerly,[9] and this is welcome news. In my study of 1980-81, cooperative outreach programs were a top-ranked item for all participants in the study, gerontologists as well as librarians. This suggests that our overtures will be well-received. But we must take the first step, because we are very likely to be overlooked unless we do.

*Guideline 4: Provide library service appropriate to the special needs of all older adults including the minority who are geographically isolated, homebound, institutionalized, or disabled.* This guideline emphasizes ALL older adults, but it is in the area of the group here called the "minority" that historically we have succeeded, at least to a measure. Deposit collections in homes for the aging and bookmobile services, in which we take the collection to our clientele, have been some of our most-cited services to elders. We have emphasized services to the disabled as well. But the fact that these services are to a *minority* of the elderly has, curiously, worked to hinder other programs especially targetted to the elderly.

As mentioned earlier, many librarians are influenced by a belief that elders who are active and well do not want to be singled out for special treatment; this is a product of a society that praises youthfulness and strong bodies. As the elderly increase in numbers, it is likely that this concept will diminish, among librarians and also among elders who cling to this notion.

Just as we have long targeted young adults, for example, our aging clientele have particular interests and needs relative to their lives, too. Older adults typically have more leisure time than the younger generations, and they are relaxed about their informational needs. Elderhostel, for example, has succeeded in part because the program has taken into account the differences. Elders are not so likely to be striving with the all of their time; the ambitious needs of a younger generation have fallen away to a more balanced life style. The Humanities Program of the National Council on the Aging, like the Elderhostel Program, has worked well. As examples, then, of the right kind of targetted program, we might look to these two examples. Neither of these programs questioned the fitness of designing programs specifically for the elder. Yet, tellingly, neither of these two highly successful programs have been library-bound, even though the content would suggest their linkage to the library.

Three premier programs for the aging have nation-wide recognizability in the library world: the Brooklyn Public Library's Service to the Aging (SAGE); Miami-Dade Public Library's "60 PLus" Club; and the Cleveland Public Library's "Live Long and Like It" Club.

These are nationally-recognized examples of what we and others can do. Is it not time for the library world to come up with more outstanding examples?

In short, it is right and good that special needs of older adults be satisfied in library programs that are specifically designed for older adults.

*Guideline 11: Incorporate as part of the library's planning and evaluation process the changing needs of an aging population.* This guideline emphasizes with the term, "changing needs," the "graying" of the population. It is virtually impossible to read any article discussing the needs of older people without encountering a statistical profile emphasizing that their numbers are larger, both percentage-wise and in the aggregate, and these figures are expected to climb into the next century rapidly. The "graying" should be a call for action on our part.

We may take into account the research cited earlier in determining that what we have done is lamentably little. But we cannot allow this to continue if we are to do our job right. Reference services and programs to elders will become more and more important as the years go by. As elders increase in numbers, their advocacy will increase, and other agencies will step in to provide the services, probably for a fee. The library is uniquely suited for providing the informational undergirding of our society—a role that sometimes only librarians take seriously. We need to move with the times, energetically embracing the information age that so many are talking about. This speaks to elders as well, even if they have not been lifelong users heretofore. Let us budget our money, as little as it might feel that it is, to provide for the informational needs of this increasingly able and active generation of older adults.

## CONCLUSION

Acting upon these guidelines will not help every elderly person who has the need for greater access to information, because there are constraints in funding and personnel that make the issues bigger than can be addressed conclusively. But we can make a new beginning, and that effort might turn out to be far better than we might hope now. Librarians have given services to the older adult "lip service" for far too long; let us work together to see that this unfortunate situation is amended.

## REFERENCES

1. "Guidelines for Library Service to Older Adults," *RQ* 26 (4) (Summer 1987), pp. 444-447.
2. Cleveland Public Library, *National Survey of Library Services to the Aging*, Final Report. Arlington, VA: ERIC Document Reproduction Service, ED 067 521 and ED 072 835, 1971 and 1973.
3. Turock, Betty, "Public Library Service for Older Adults: Update 1984," *Library Quarterly*, 57 (2) (April 1987), pp. 137-170.
4. Hales, Celia, "How Should the Information Needs of the Aging Be Met? A Delphi Response," *The Gerontologist* 25 (2) (April 1985), pp. 172-176.
5. Hales-Mabry, Celia, "How Should the Information Needs of the Aging Be Met?" Arlington, VA: ERIC Document Reproduction Service, ED 294 582, 1988.
6. "Guidelines for Library Service to Older Adults" is available for $1.00 prepaid from the Reference and Adult Services Division (RASD), American Library Association, 50 E. Huron Street, Chicago, IL 60611. Enclose a self-addressed, stamped envelope. See above for original publication in *RQ*.
7. Turock, "Public Library Service for Older Adults: Update 1986," Final

Report, July 15, 1987, Rutgers University, School of Communication, Information and Library Studies, p. 33.

8. Simon, Cheryl, "A Care Package," *Psychology Today* 22 (4) (April 1988), pp. 42-49.

9. Moore, Bessie Boehm, and Young, Christina Carr, "Library/Information Services and the Nation's Elderly," *Journal of the American Society for Information Science*, 36 (6), pp. 364-368.

# The Invisible Client:
# Meeting the Needs of Persons
# with Learning Disabilities

## Darlene E. Weingand

**SUMMARY.** Persons with learning disabilities comprise an invisible client group and are often overlooked in the reference process. While a learning disability is not a form of mental retardation or an emotional disorder [as has been often believed in the past], it is a permanent disorder which affects the manner in which individuals with normal or above average intelligence take in, retain and express information. Consequently, the information needs of these potential clients must be approached by means of both different reference strategies and a sensitivity to the special attributes of this client group.

The library, regardless of type and mission, is a very special place. It is a window to the world of information, education, recreation and culture. In its role as access portal, it brings people and knowledge together, enhancing the quality of life for both individuals and society. Yet, there is a group of potential library clients whose information needs, while as real and vital as any, are often poorly served by the reference process. These are the invisible clients: persons with learning disabilities.

Learning disabilities are not disfiguring, and generally are not diagnosed before a child reaches school age. Though learning disabilities can range from mild to severe, the majority of LD [learning disabled] children have mild to moderate problems. Even a mild

Darlene E. Weingand is Associate Professor, School of Library and Information Studies, University of Wisconsin-Madison, 600 North Park Street, Madison, WI 53706.

learning disability, however, can cause major problems for the individual. Misdiagnosis [lazy, dull, retarded] of LD children is still prevalent. They are still an enigma—the bright child who cannot read, the average child who cannot write or do arithmetic, the child whose academic work is acceptable, but who fails physical education because of "clumsiness."[1]

The issues concerning learning disabilities are of national concern. According to the U.S. Department of Education, about 1.75 million school-age children have learning disabilities. Recognized estimates project approximately 3 percent of the children in the United States as being learning disabled.[2] However, these statistics do not reflect the current picture of adult persons with learning disabilities.[3]

Today, libraries are becoming increasingly aware of the special needs of particular client groups. Both the sensitivities of library staff and the power of law have combined to create library environments that are accessible to persons with physical disabilities relating to movement, vision, and other dysfunctions. However, educators in the last decade have become aware of another set of disabilities—learning disabilities—that are not obvious to the eye and have been heretofore attributed to other causes, such as mental retardation and/or emotional disorders. Because learning disabilities cannot be overtly observed by librarians, the special needs of these clients have been essentially invisible. Moreover, the lack of response to these needs over time has, in many instances, "turned off" many clients to library use.

Yet we are in an information society, and all citizens require access to information in order to successfully cope with a changing world. As the U.S. Department of Education has stated:

> The Information Age has swept around the world like a poorly forecast winter storm; its swirling blizzard of facts, figures and data has been as bewildering as it has been challenging. This is the nature of the Information Age, but unlike the snows of February, it is here to stay. The necessity is for all of us to become acclimatized to it.
>
> As never before, issues pile up; spawned by awesome technology or by political and social ferment in every corner of the

earth. These are issues without easy answers, and some of them may affect human survival. So, they have to be understood; decisions must be made about them. To be responsible, rational citizens in this new time, we must chart a stable persistent course through the waves of clues, tidbits, hard facts, and rumors.

This can be done, as *A Nation at Risk* eloquently urged, if we move aggressively to create a Learning Society. "*To do so calls for forming an alliance among teachers, education administrators, parents and other citizens, and the nation's librarians. Through their united efforts, these men and women will be able to provide interrelated, lifelong educational experiences for people of all ages and in all walks of life. Only through this joint activity can a workable Learning Society be realized.*"[4] [Italics added]

This quotation specifically calls for cooperative efforts between librarians and a variety of other concerned groups in order to meet the informational and educational needs of all citizens. However, as stated earlier, the invisible clients—persons with learning disabilities—have been largely overlooked. Further, although schools are now identifying students with these special needs, there are millions of adults who have not had access to this special attention since they have long been removed from the school situation. In addition, when the LD student enters the adult world, support systems suddenly disappear, and libraries become the sole access point for further education and information-seeking. This "shortfall" of opportunity for a major segment of the population must be a primary concern of libraries of all types.

## *WHAT ARE LEARNING DISABILITIES?*

A learning disability can be described as follows:

- A *permanent disorder* which affects the manner in which individuals with normal or above average intelligence take in, retain and express information. Like interference on the radio or a fuzzy TV picture, incoming or outgoing information may become scrambled as it travels between the eye, ear or skin, and the brain;

- Commonly recognized in LD individuals as *deficits* in one or more of the following areas: reading comprehension, spelling, written expression, math computation, and problem solving. Less frequent, but no less troublesome, are problems in organizational skills, time management, and social skills. Many LD persons may also have language-based and/or perceptual problems;

- Often *inconsistent*. It may present problems on Mondays, but not on Tuesdays. It may cause problems throughout grade school, seem to disappear during high school, and then resurface again in college. It may manifest itself in only one specific academic area, such as math or foreign language;

- *Frustrating*! Persons with learning disabilities often have to deal not only with functional limitations, but also with the frustration of having to "prove" that their invisible disabilities may be as handicapping as paraplegia.[5]

Visual/perceptual problems can occur in terms of visual discrimination, visual sequencing, visual memory, and the speed of processing information. Commonly used descriptors include: Dyslexia . . . difficulty with reading/writing; Dyscalcula . . . difficulty with calculating and math; and Dysgraphia . . . difficulty with handwriting.

Auditory perception problems involve difficulty with accurately interpreting information gathered through the ears, differentiating between similar sounds, concentrating, picking up the main message or "tuning in." These problems can affect social interaction.

Temporal/spacial problems involve getting lost or getting places on time. Tactile defensiveness may result in not wanting to be touched and difficulty in differentiating between textures. In the language area, there may be difficulty with word retrieval—which may be accompanied by a compensating use of gestures.

It is clear that there is a wide range of potential disabilities—which adds yet more argument to the contention that libraries must provide a corollary broad range of materials and services in order to meet these specialized needs.

## COMMON CHARACTERISTICS
## OF LEARNING DISABLED PERSONS

Since a variety of skills can be impacted, no two persons with learning disabilities will be affected in exactly the same way. Possible characteristics include the following:

- *Reading Skills*

  - Slow reading rate and/or difficulty in modifying reading rate in accordance with material difficulty.
  - Poor comprehension and retention.
  - Difficulty identifying important points and themes.
  - Poor mastery of phonics, confusion of similar words, difficulty integrating new vocabulary.

- *Written Language Skills*

  - Difficulty with sentence structure [e.g., incomplete sentences, run-on's, poor use of grammar, missing inflectional endings].
  - Frequent spelling errors [e.g., omissions, substitutions, transpositions], especially in specialized and foreign vocabulary.
  - Inability to copy correctly from a book or the blackboard.
  - Slow writer.
  - Poor penmanship [e.g., poorly-formed letters, incorrect use of capitalization, trouble with spacing, overly-large handwriting].

- *Oral Language Skills*

  - Inability to concentrate on and comprehend oral language.
  - Difficulty in orally expressing ideas which s/he seems to understand.
  - Written expression is better than oral expression.
  - Difficulty speaking grammatically correct English.
  - Cannot tell a story in proper sequence.

- *Mathematical Skills*

  - Incomplete mastery of basic facts [e.g., mathematical tables].

—Reverses numbers [e.g., 123 to 321 or 231].
—Confuses operational symbols, especially + and ×.
—Copies problems incorrectly from one line to another.
—Difficulty recalling the sequence of operational processes.
—Inability to understand and retain abstract concepts.
—Difficulty comprehending word problems.
—Reasoning deficits.

• *Organizational and Study Skills*

—Time management difficulties.
—Slow to start and complete tasks.
—Repeated inability, on a day-to-day basis, to recall what has been taught.
—Difficulty following oral and written directions.
—Lack of overall organization in written notes and compositions.
—Demonstrates short attention span during lectures/instructions.
—Inefficient use of library reference materials.

• *Social Skills*

—For the same reason that a person with visual perceptual problems may have trouble discriminating between the letters "b" and "d," s/he may be unable to detect the difference between a joking wink and a disgusted glance.
—People with auditory perceptual problems might not notice the difference between sincere and sarcastic comments, or be able to recognize other subtle changes in tone of voice.
—These difficulties in interpreting nonverbal messages may result in lowered self-esteem and may cause individuals to have trouble meeting people, working cooperatively with others, and making friends.[6]

## ONE LIBRARY'S APPROACH: THE WESTCHESTER LIBRARY SYSTEM

In 1984, the Westchester Library System in New York State received a grant from the Foundations for Children with Learning Disabilities to explore and develop ways in which librarians could become more responsive to the needs of learning disabled children, their families, and the professionals who work with them. The grant involved in-service training sessions for the children's librarians in the thirty-eight member public libraries in Westchester County, the establishment of replicable pilot projects, and the development of printed resource materials.[7]

Simulation education was included in the in-service training in order to increase librarians' sensitivity to the special needs of children with learning disabilities. Examination of books was modified to include an awareness of content, design and format. The pilot projects varied in both scope and content: sample projects involved special book/media collections; purchase of books and matching cassette versions; parent education programs; and the use of the computer in word processing and creative writing.[8]

Westchester County's grant results illustrate the important role that libraries can play in providing a non-judgmental, non-threatening, educational and entertaining environment in which persons with learning disabilities and their friends and relatives can engage in the pursuit of knowledge and recreation. Sharing books, films and videos, puppet shows, recordings and games can add to personal enjoyment and enhance the quality of life — provided the library contains the necessary resources. It is incumbent upon library administrations to recognize this serious responsibility to supply a wide variety of materials and services and allocate available funds in order to achieve this goal.

## *STRATEGIES FOR REFERENCE ASSISTANCE: CHILDREN*

Identification of children with learning disabilities can be extremely difficult for librarians who are not trained in such diagnosis. Therefore, a mandate for cooperation with teachers and counsellors in the local schools is definitely present. Once identification of these special children has been made, the next step is to focus on each child's strengths. By focusing on a child's abilities and qualities, library assistance can be tailored to complement these strengths. Areas to explore include:

- Acquired skills: What does the child already know how to do? What are the academic skills, learning competencies?
- Personal interests: What kinds of things excite the child? What hobbies, sports, books, movies, games does s/he like?
- Special talents: What actual or potential talents does the child have? Consider musical, artistic, athletic, scientific, and mechanical abilities.
- Positive qualities: What inner characteristics does the child display? Is s/he compassionate, patient, loyal, generous?[9]

In addition to the focus on individual strengths, other strategies may also prove useful to the reference librarian:

- Learn more about developmental ages relative to social, language, chronological, motor, emotional, physical and neurological development.
- Recognize the value of storytelling and the importance of reading to children; children must hear good language in order to be able to emulate it and create their own language structures.
- Consider the importance of learning styles: there are auditory, visual, and kinesthetic learners—each of which respond to a different type of materials format.
- Consciously provide information in a broad range of formats in order to meet the needs of diverse learning styles.

## *STRATEGIES FOR REFERENCE ASSISTANCE: ADULTS*

There are two fundamental approaches to working with adult persons with learning disabilities. The first, and perhaps most difficult, approach corresponds to a marketing perspective to library service: target clients are identified, their needs are assessed, and products are designed to meet those needs. Intrinsic to this approach are the communication and distribution mechanisms that will both inform and facilitate the connection between learners and services. This is no small task when the client group is one that may have given up on library service years earlier. However, it is a challenge that must be met if the library is to serve as the access to information for these clients. A community survey that asks about preferred formats for learning can help to identify this special target market.

The second approach involves the implementation of services that will meet client needs once the connection has been made. Strategies for working with learning disabled clients [regardless of age] may include:

- Study aids [for in-library and/or circulating use], including four-track, variable-speed tape recorders; talking calculators; large-print electric typewriters; magnifiers; variable speech control modules; braille dictionaries and materials; a Kurzweil Reading Machine.
- A wide variety of formats, including both audio and visual versions of information sources.
- In-library use of audiovisual equipment.
- Audio and/or video library instruction set-ups.
- Use of color coding and graphics.
- Creation of listening/viewing rooms.
- Public use of a computer terminal with word processing software. Using a computer is a multi-sensory experience — the tactile feedback of pressing the keyboard, the auditory feedback provided by the sound of clicking keys or a voice synthesizer, and the visual display of the monitor — which is frequently beneficial to a learning disabled user. In addition, the "spell-checker" has been a boon for these users.
- Extended loan periods.
- Programs, such as tutoring, assertiveness training, study skills groups.
- Use of volunteers for tutoring, reading for taping, storytelling, assisting with projects, and so forth.
- In-service training of library staff concerning the needs of clients with learning disabilities.
- Sensitivity to criteria in reviewing print materials, including attention to print size, organization, page design, format, clarity and use of language, and explicit information.

## BIBLIOTHERAPY

Another approach that librarians might employ in assisting persons with learning disabilities [or any client, for that matter] is bibliotherapy. The therapy in bibliotherapy denotes a three-step hypothesis and proceeds from identification to catharsis to insight.[10]

*Identification* with characters, situations, or elements of plot is the first step in the process and helps the reader/listener realize that s/he is not the first person to encounter a particular problem. This realization enables him/her to vicariously experience an event and helps to view the problem from a different perspective, promoting personal growth.

The second step, *catharsis*, equates with a purging or release of tension/stress. Through the vicarious experience described above, the reader/listener identifies with the characters and lives events through the unfolding of the story, gratifying personal desires. Finally, *insight* is the final step during which the reader/listener internalizes new awarenesses and modifies present attitudes and behaviors.

Librarians, with their knowledge of the materials in the collection, have unique opportunities to employ the process of bibliotherapy to enable learning disabled clients to work through the normal frustrations of life — and the special frustrations that disability has presented to them. Bibliotherapy can be particularly valuable in promoting a positive self-image and overcoming feelings of inferiority and failure — feelings which often accompany the sense of being "different."

While no strategy can be applied to all situations, bibliotherapy can be an important addition to the tools that the librarian can use in responding to the needs of these special clients.

## FOR FURTHER DISCUSSION

It is important to emphasize that libraries have not been expressly negligent in providing materials and services for persons with learning disabilities. A scarce two decades ago, primary and secondary education was just beginning to become aware of learning disabilities as a special area of concern. But it is equally important to stress that these invisible clients have a right to equal access to information and that libraries have a responsibility to create that access to the greatest possible extent.

In an acknowledgment of this mandate for service, the following questions are proposed for further thought, discussion and action:[11]

- What is your community's/institution's attitude toward persons with learning disabilities?
- What support systems are in place? What could and should be in place?
- What can libraries in your community do to create access to information and education for learners with each type of learning disability? What can be done to foster cooperation among potential resource groups and individuals?
- Are children read to in school? in the home? in the library? How can this be encouraged?
- What can be done to provide learning materials in schools, homes and libraries that will respond to the diverse learning styles of children and adults?
- Are there locally "famous" individuals who are learning disabled who would be willing to publically serve as role models for others in the community?
- Are tutoring services available in the community? Is the library involved?
- Are there any sources of funding in the community that could provide "seed money" for special projects?
- What creative artists reside in the community that could add variety and color to storytelling events at the library?
- Is storytelling restricted to preschool ages, or can programs be developed for schoolage children, teens and adults?
- Could special programmatic activities, such as a "Media Fair," be staged at the library and produced by cooperating agencies and businesses within the community?
- What mechanism can be created to develop an enthusiastic, effective and conscientious roster of volunteers?

# REFERENCES

1. Alaine Lane. *Readings in Microcomputers and Learning Disabilities* (Guilford, CT: Special Learning Corporation, 1984), p. 3.

2. Foundation for Children with Learning Disabilities. *The FCLD Guide for Parents of Children with Learning Disabilities* (New York: Education Systems, Inc., 1984), p. 8.

3. Learning disabilities have only been identified and tracked during the past twenty years; therefore, statistics on adults are a matter of conjecture.

4. Taken from *Alliance for Excellence: Librarians Respond to A Nation at Risk* (U.S. Department of Education, July 1984).

5. Taken from a brochure entitled "College Students with Learning Disabilities" produced by the University of Wisconsin-Madison McBurney Resource Center, 1983.

6. Taken from a brochure entitled "College Students with Learning Disabilities" produced by the University of Wisconsin-Madison McBurney Resource Center, 1983.

7. Judith Rovenger. "Learning Differences/Library Directions: Library Service to Children with Learning Differences," *Library Trends*, (Winter 1987): 428-429.

8. Rovenger, "Learning Differences/Library Directions . . .," 429-430.

9. Thomas Armstrong. "How Real are Learning Disabilities?" *Learning 85*, 14 (September 1985): 46.

10. Barbara E. Lenkowsky and Ronald S. Lenkowsky. "Bibliotherapy for the LD Adolescent," in Carol H. Thomas and James L. Thomas, eds. *Meeting the Needs of the Handicapped: A Resource for Teachers and Librarians* (Phoenix, AZ: Oryx press, 1980), p. 123.

11. The term "community" is used here to denote the market area to which the library directs service. For the special library, it is the corporation/institution; for the media center, it is the school; for the academic library, it is the college/university; and for the public library, it is the municipality.

# The Reference Librarian as Audience for NLS Reference Publications

## Philip W. Wong-Cross

**SUMMARY.** The author describes the collections, roles, and services of the Reference Section of the National Library Service for the Blind and Physically Handicapped (NLS), Library of Congress. He suggests that there is an audience among reference librarians for the publications produced by the NLS Reference Section. The reference librarians of the NLS network of regional and subregional libraries serving visually impaired and physically disabled readers are, of course, a primary audience for NLS reference publications. However, all items may be used as well by other librarians serving visually impaired and physically disabled people, the majority of whom undoubtedly work in public libraries. The author argues that as reference tools these publications may be used to answer quite specific inquiries and to make sound referrals on a wide range of questions. Librarians may request individual titles or have their libraries placed on a mailing list for any of the cited series.

## THE NATIONAL LIBRARY SERVICE FOR THE BLIND AND PHYSICALLY HANDICAPPED (NLS)

The National Library Service for the Blind and Physically Handicapped (NLS), Library of Congress, produces general-interest recorded and braille books and magazines for eligible blind and physically disabled readers in the United States and for eligible American citizens living abroad. Eligible readers are those who, because of temporary or permanent visual impairment or physical

Philip W. Wong-Cross is Head, Reference Section National Library Service for the Blind and Physically Handicapped, Library of Congress, Washington, DC 20542.

disability, are unable to read standard print or hold or turn the pages of standard printed books. The recorded and braille materials are distributed to readers through the NLS network of approximately 160 regional and subregional libraries nationwide. American citizens living abroad are served directly by NLS. In addition to literary materials, NLS also produces special-format music materials, including music scores in braille and large print, and music magazines and books about music and musicians in large-print, braille, and recorded formats. NLS music patrons are served directly by NLS.

Additional information about the history and development of the National Library Service for the Blind and Physically Handicapped, Library of Congress, may be found in the monograph *That All May Read*, cited in the "References" at the end of this article.

## A VARIED CLIENTELE

The NLS Reference Section serves a varied clientele. It serves as the library for NLS staff, as the reference and referral center of final resort (in the section's areas of specialization) for NLS network regional and subregional libraries, and as a major reference resource for researchers on library service to special groups, particularly on the history and current practice of library and other services and programs for visually impaired and physically disabled people. In addition to answering written correspondence, telephone and in-person inquiries, the NLS Reference Section publishes a wide variety of reference publications.

This article concentrates on the reference librarian as an audience for NLS Reference Section publications. While some items are produced primarily for distribution to NLS network libraries and are therefore produced in limited quantities, all items listed are intended for librarians serving visually impaired and physically disabled persons, the largest number of whom, outside of the NLS network, undoubtedly work in public libraries. This article will further concentrate on the uses of those titles that are currently available and that can be obtained by writing or calling the NLS Reference Section.

## NLS REFERENCE COLLECTIONS

The NLS reference collections consist of several thousand current and retrospective book titles and approximately five hundred periodical titles. The section also houses an extensive vertical file of more than a thousand folders, and several discrete information files (each file consisting of several hundred folders) on: national consumer and advocacy organizations; sources of large print, braille, recorded, and other special-format materials; sources for adapted computer hardware and software, assistive devices for reading, writing, and other communication, as well as toys and games adapted for visually impaired or physically disabled children; and finally, sources of audiovisual materials that accurately and constructively depict visually impaired persons and those with other physical disabilities.

These collections are used by reference section staff to respond to inquiries on such topics as:

- library services to visually impaired and physically disabled readers
- sources of commercial spoken-word recordings and large-print publications
- assistive devices for reading, writing, and other communication
- computer applications for braille and voice output and other adaptive technologies
- national information, consumer, and advocacy organizations of and for visually impaired and physically disabled persons
- research and technology having application to training, employment, and independent living for disabled persons
- information and referral on statistics about disabling conditions
- social issues that affect visually impaired and physically disabled persons

Along with the books, periodicals, and other print resources (newspaper clippings, brochures, catalogs), the Reference Section accesses a wide range of computerized databases including the MUMS/SCORPIO databases of the Library of Congress, those generally available through DIALOG and BRS, and a number of specialized subject-area databases, such as APH/CARL of the American Printing House for the Blind, and REHABDATA (also available through BRS) of the National Rehabilitation Information Center. Additional information on online resources in the blindness field may be found in the recent article by Leslie Rosen cited in the "References" at the end of this article.

## PUBLICATIONS SERIES

First a word about the series of publications available from the NLS Reference Section, and then more detail about specific titles and their use as reference tools. The NLS Reference Section produces the following types of publications on an ongoing basis:

"Package Library" — Each package library consists of a collection of items including article reprints, brochures, pamphlets, resource lists, and select bibliographies on a single broad topic.

"Reference Circular" — Each title in this series is a compilation of current information on a topic of wide interest to disabled persons and those who provide services to them. Titles are revised from time to time, as deemed appropriate, to reflect the most recent information on a topic.

"Reference Bibliography" — A series of citations to the literature on topics of interest to students, professionals, and others doing research on some aspect of handicapping conditions or on services to disabled people.

*Added Entries* — A quarterly list of significant new publications added to the NLS reference collections.

*Library Resources for the Blind and Physically Handicapped* — An annual directory of libraries in the U.S. that provide reading materials to visually impaired and other print-handicapped readers. Includes the addresses of all NLS network libraries and other national resources for reading materials in special format. Contains annual statistics for the entire NLS network covering budgets, staffs, collections, readership and circulation.

A mailing list is maintained for each of the series above with the exception of the "Package Library." Because package libraries are issued in limited quantities for primary distribution to NLS network libraries, they are available to others in single copies only, as long as the supply lasts.

## REFERENCE SECTION PUBLICATIONS

The publications most likely to be useful on an ongoing basis to public library reference librarians are the *reference circulars* and *reference bibliographies*. Reference Section publications are citations to the standard print literature and are, for the most part, published in standard print. However, if a reference circular or bibliography is considered of direct interest and usefulness to the NLS reader, it will also be produced, funds permitting, in braille or recorded formats. Though these publications are created in sufficient quantity to be distributed in response to general inquiries about a topic, each is also a reference tool in the hand of the astute reference librarian in search of a fact to answer a specific inquiry or to make a sound referral.

The *modus operandi* for familiarizing the reader with these publications is to comment upon each available title in turn: first, reference circulars, then reference bibliographies, alphabetically by title. If a title seems less than useful, skip to the next one. But, as titles never give the whole story, be cautious as you skip!

Several titles cited below are somewhat dated (*caveat emptor!*), but are considered by many librarians in the NLS network to be of continued usefulness and are, therefore, still available for distribution.

## REFERENCE CIRCULARS

Reference circulars are compiled with information supplied by producers and distributors in response to surveys conducted by the Reference Section. When a topic is first covered, a survey tool is created and sent to all identified sources of information. When an updated edition of an existing circular is to be compiled, all earlier cited sources, and all new additional sources are surveyed for their most recent information. We also ask to be placed on organizations' mailing lists in order to continue to receive updated information.

*Bibles, Other Scriptures, Liturgies, and Hymnals in Special Media* (1988) identifies the sources for braille, large-print and recorded formats for items in each of the categories listed in the title. This circular covers more than fifteen versions of the Christian Bible and the sacred texts of Judaism, Buddhism, Hinduism, and Islam. It also covers sources of scriptures in sixteen languages, and one source (Lutheran Braille Workers, Inc.) that produces titles in thirty-three languages. Note that even the lengthy title doesn't tell it all: several concordances and a commentary are also included in this circular.

*Braille Instruction and Writing Equipment* (1986) lists braille instruction manuals and braille reading manuals (a distinction to think about); courses for blind and visually impaired as well as sighted students; and all sorts of equipment for writing, erasing, filing, and labeling brailled materials. By the way, sighted readers generally read braille with their eyes rather than their fingers, a surprise initially to each and every sighted braille enthusiast.

*Building a Library Collection on Blindness and Physical Handicaps: Basic Materials and Resources* (1985) is in the process of being updated. This title is useful for its lengthy bibliography of books on subjects ranging from accessibility to rehabilitation. Issues in education, employment, independent living, the psychosocial aspects of disability, and recreation are all covered along with many other topics. (This is a case of a short subtitle as understatement!) In addition to the lengthy bibliography, there are listings of directories, periodicals, sources of free and inexpensive materials (often found in the vertical file collections of public libraries), information centers, and online services for the librarian seeking disability-related materials and resources.

*From School to Working Life: Resources and Services* (1985) will assist librarians helping disabled students preparing for the transition from high school to working life. Arranged according to the concept of three transition models presented in the paper "Bridges from School to Working Life" by Madeleine Will, Assistant Secretary for Special Education and Rehabilitative Services, U.S. Department of Education, in 1984, this circular identifies resources and services under each of her models. "Transition without Special Services" is made by the disabled students using their "own resources or those generally available to all citizens" and includes sources of financial aid for college students, disabled students' rights, and a list of books in special media on career planning. "Transition with Time-Limited Services" are for those individuals who "use specialized, time-limited services like vocational rehabilitation, post-secondary vocational education, and other job-training programs to gain entry into the labor market." This section of the circular covers job training, placement and career matching services, employment networks, and information and referral centers; cites available federal programs; and lists divisions of rehabilitation for each state. This section concludes with a list of the key provisions of the Randolph-Sheppard Vending Facility Program. "Transition with Ongoing Services (Supported Employment Programs)" covers transition that requires ongoing support for the employee. National programs and several model programs at the local level are described. The circular concludes with a section on "Services and Opportunities Relating to All Three Transition Models," which covers issues of job accommodation through assistive technology and the provisions for nondiscrimination, affirmative action, and reasonable accommodation of "The Rehabilitation Act of 1973."

Talking Books have long been available through NLS to eligible visually impaired and physically disabled readers. A series of circulars on the availability of commercial sources for spoken-word recordings was compiled to identify reading materials to supplement the NLS collections, and to anticipate the desire for cassette reading materials on the part of the general public. There were four titles in the series in the early 1980s. With the burgeoning market for recorded materials and the proliferation of titles, there are now several large trade bibliographies on the medium of the audio cassette. Examples are: *Words on Cassette 1987/88: A Comprehensive Bibliography of Spoken Word Audiocassettes* (R.R. Bowker) and *Words on Tape 1987/88: An International Guide to the Audio Cassette Market* (Meckler Corporation). There are, however, still two titles in the NLS spoken-word series, listing information in areas of interest to NLS readers and to librarians serving them. The NLS reference circular *Guide to Spoken-Word Recordings: Popular Literature* (1987) lists sources of recorded cassettes, recorded discs, and combinations (recorded material accompanied by print equivalents) of literary works in most genres for children and adults. A select list of publications on recorded materials and playback equipment is included. The other extant circular in the series is the *Guide to Spoken-Word Recordings: Foreign-Language Instruction and Literature* (1988) which covers sources for an amazing array of languages from Afrikaans (South Africa) to Chinyanja (spoken language of Malawi); Hausa, Igbo, and Yoruba (all of Nigeria); from Latin (ancient Rome, and its provinces; and in some times and places, the Roman Catholic Church) to Twi (Ghana); from Urdu (Pakistan) to Yiddish (almost everywhere, at one time or another). Separate indexes by language for instruction sources and for literature sources make for ease of access to desired information.

Ever-increasing numbers of disabled persons are traveling far and wide. The librarian in need of travel information (accessible facilities, available local transportation, special tours, travel agencies) will find the diminutive circular *Information for Handicapped Travelers* (1987) a good referral tool. This circular includes print and special-format books for the inexperienced as well as for the seasoned traveler. Information centers included provide a variety of services from the issuance of special discount travel cards for the legally blind to arranging for immunizations and medical care in foreign countries; from maintaining a clearinghouse of exchange-visit opportunities for disabled travelers to making referrals to appropriate organizations and travel agencies that specialize in working with disabled travelers.

*National Organizations Concerned with Visually and Physically Handicapped Persons* (1983) also is in the process of being updated and replaced by a *series* of circulars on national information and advocacy organizations for each particular disabling condition or groups of conditions. This edition of the circular is divided into two parts. The first, and larger, section is a listing of nongovernmental organizations. The second part is a list of federal agencies with varying responsibilities in the area of disabilities programs and enforcement issues. This circular remains useful for identifying the types of activities and the names of publications of the nongovernmental organizations listed. It has aided libraries and other organizations in locating state and local affiliates for the national-level listings. The federal government listings are, in this 1983 edition, for the most part too dated to be useful and should be used with considerable wariness, if at all. A current directory of U.S. government agencies should be consulted for the entries given here. Look for updates to this circular beginning shortly.

*Parents Guide to the Development of Pre-School Handicapped Children: Resources and Services* (1984) was compiled to assist parents of preschool children in identifying materials for early childhood development. The circular lists a wide range of recorded "directed learning" activities, stories, and songs available from commercial sources, as well as educational games, toys, and play equipment that have been adapted for children with disabilities. A short select bibliography of books for parents, a listing of magazines of interest to parents, and a list of national organizations concerned with handicapped children completes this circular.

While large-print literary materials are not produced by the National Library Service for the Blind and Physically Handicapped, NLS network regional and subregional libraries receive inquiries about the availability of such material and many do purchase and deliver large-print books as part of their library service. *Reading Materials in Large Type* (1987) is compiled to assist network libraries in identifying sources of large-print reading materials. This circular is in three parts. Part I, "Producers and Distributors of Large-Type Materials," lists sources of large-print materials, including many foreign sources. For each source, a note is given on the subjects or literary genres available from that source. Part II, "Selected Large-Type Materials for Reference and Special Needs," lists sources of selected large print-books (and magazines) under broad headings such as "Adjustment to Visual Loss," "Classics," "Dictionaries and Encyclopedias" and "Music." Part III, "Further Information about Large-Type Materials and Services," lists trade and special-audience bibliographies such as R.R. Bowker's *Large Type Books in Print* (now entitled *The Complete Directory of Large Print Books and Serials*), and the NLS directory, *Volunteers Who Produce Books*, respectively.

The reference circular *Reading, Writing, and Other Communica-*

*tion Aids for Visually and Physically Handicapped Persons* (1986) lists a wide range of assistive devices for reading, writing, and other communication. This sixty-nine page circular contains more information than can be listed in this short space except in the broadest of terms. For being the comprehensive reference tool that it is, with more than 300 assistive devices listed, this circular and its contents can be only hinted at by its title, its table of contents, and even its index. Only searching by the skilled reference professional will bring out all there is in this reference circular to answer the wide variety of questions it is designed to address. In it are listed bookholders, page turners, lapboards, bookstands, lampstands, and wheelchair trays. Braille reading and writing aids, communication aids for multiply disabled individuals, low-vision aids, and reading machines, speech synthesizers, speech software, and talking terminals. Optical enlargers, photoenlargers, and software for computer enlarging. Sound reproducers, recorders, and accessories. This circular is complete with subject and brand-name index for increased access to the myriad devices listed.

*Reference Books in Special Media* (1982) and *Reference Books in Special Media: Addendum* (1987) both list the most recent editions, at the time of compilation, of reference works in braille, large-print, cassette, and recorded disc formats. Both editions contain a title index. Access to reference books has been greatly enhanced by electronic publishing trends and with appropriate personal computer applications, making this title more obsolete by the day. In the meanwhile, if you have a title in mind, one that is not too current, you will likely find it listed in one of these circulars.

*Sources of Audiovisual Materials about Handicapping Conditions* (1985) cites sources that depict disabled persons in an accurate and constructive light and disabling conditions free of negative stereotyping. The media covered include films, filmstrips, videocassettes, and slides. In the first section of this circular, "Audiovisual Materials for Adults," the producers and distributors are listed under broad subject categories from "Accessibility" to "Volunteers." "Audiovisual Materials for Children," the next section, is similarly arranged for materials suitable for children. The third section gives for each distributor: the medium; whether the material is for purchase, loan, or rental; and the subjects covered by each producer or distributor. This infrequently requested (is there still A/V anxiety out there?) reference circular contains a wealth of information.

*Sources of Braille Reading Materials* (1985) lists sources of braille available for loan, purchase, rental, or free (i.e., giveaway) distribution. Divided into four sections, the circular gives in addition to sources of standard braille reading materials, sources of specialized braille, such as "Jumbo Braille" (oversized), "PRINT/ BRAILLE" (combinations of print and braille texts), "Tactile Books for Children" (in fact, *not* braille, but more reasonably listed here than in any other circular because of its *tactility*), and "Versabraille Books" (paperless! braille). Finally, to complete the picture, the names of producers of quantity braille (50- to 1,000-copy runs) are given, and the names of information resources and organizations promoting the use of braille are included and may be contacted for further information.

*Sports, Games, and Outdoor Recreation for Handicapped Persons* (1983) covers sports from "All Terrain Vehicles" through Boating, Fishing, Flying, Scuba Diving, and Waterskiing to Wrestling, with almost everything in between. Section I is divided between organizations that promote a single sport and those that promote multi-sport activities. Cross references are made between the two groups and types of organizations. Competitions (national and international) are listed, followed by sources for specially adapted or specially designed equipment for the sports covered. Section II covers camping facilities (for traditional-minded campers) and wilderness training, which includes whitewater rafting and tobogganing (for the more adventuresome-minded). Section III lists sources for some twenty table games from backgammon to Scrabble and tic tac toe. A brief section on clearinghouses of information on sports and the disabled and a list of periodicals on recreation complete this circular.

## REFERENCE BIBLIOGRAPHIES

Reference bibliographies are citations to the literature on a variety of topics of interest to those doing research on some aspect of handicapping conditions. These bibliographies are compiled after exhaustive searches of the available literature. But as the intended audience for these bibliographies are *practitioner* librarians rather than *researcher* librarians, the items selected for inclusion in a reference bibliography generally have application in the contemporary library setting.

*Accessibility: Designing Buildings for the Needs of Handicapped Persons* (1983) is a select, annotated bibliography of books, articles, reports, and films on barrier-free design. It is "intended as an introduction to the subject for architects, administrators, and other persons planning accessible facilities." Items cited cover legal requirements and civil rights, federal and other standards promulgated for barrier-free design, creating or renovating for accessible public space and domestic architecture, as well as accessible travel and transportation.

*Attitudes toward Handicapped People, Past and Present* (1984) is a bibliography that every librarian about to serve persons with disabilities will want to request. Items cited cover the attitudes of disabled persons themselves, their peers, their employers, and of society in general. There are articles that cover the history and development of what many may now consider quaint, strange, or even horrid attitudes; and other articles that hold up a mirror to the varied attitudes of the present. There are items that assess the effects of society's attitudes, and those that help assess one's own attitudes. A brief filmography attests to the growing numbers of audiovisuals that depict positive attitudes and non-stereotyped approaches toward disabled persons. There are, finally, items to assist librarians to break down attitudinal barriers to library service.

*Braille: History and Recent Developments* (1982), though dated, may be used in conjunction with the reference circular *Braille Instruction and Writing Equipment* (1986), cited above. The two publications give the reader a sound historical perspective and a fairly complete picture of the current status of braille instruction and technology for braille production.

*Library and Information Services to Persons with Disabilities* (1989) is a select, annotated bibliography on contemporary programs and practices in library and information services to individuals with disabilities. The introduction refers the user to *Library Literature* and to the ERIC and LISA databases for bibliographic citations prior to 1983 and for extensive coverage of this topic. Readers are also referred to *That All May Read*, the NLS monograph on the history of the National Library Service for the Blind and Physically Handicapped (full citation below, under "References").

*Mobility and Mobility Aids for Visually Handicapped Individuals* (1984) is geared to the professional, student or other interested parties researching the areas of mobility and orientation. This bibliography covers instruction and training for mobility and orientation, the research literature, mobility for special populations (including children, multiply handicapped individuals, and persons living in rural areas) and the sources for training of mobility professionals, the sources of mobility aids, and the addresses (at time of compilation) of dog guide schools. As with all circulars and bibliographies that are dated, the librarian should contact the NLS Reference Section for additional sources in any given area or for updated information for any cited resource.

*Selected Readings for Parents of Preschool Handicapped Children* (1986) cites information of concern to parents including sibling and other family member interactions with the disabled child, organizing for effective action with outside service providers, learning the legal rights of disabled persons, recognizing the need for family counseling, providing for home care as needed, and numerous other issues. This bibliography includes a listing of periodicals of general interest to parents of disabled children including *The Exceptional Parent, Future Reflections, Parents' Choice*, and others. A list of periodicals for preschool children completes this short bibliography. Additional information will be found in the reference circular *Parents Guide to the Development of Preschool Handicapped Children: Resources and Services* (see above).

## FOR MORE INFORMATION

The NLS Reference Section provides information to interested parties about any aspect of the NLS program. Requests for applications for library service and the addresses of cooperating libraries may also be obtained by contacting the Reference Section. In addition to providing information about NLS, the Reference Section answers inquiries about library services to special groups, and on a wide range of other services and subjects of concern to disabled persons, their families, and to professionals who work with them. For questions outside the scope of the NLS Reference collections, i.e., those of a strictly legal or medical nature, alternative sources are suggested and appropriate referrals made.

*To request publications or to be placed on the NLS Reference Section mailing lists —*

Single copies of any of the titles cited may be requested by writing to:

> Reference Section
> National Library Service for the Blind
>     and Physically Handicapped
> Library of Congress
> Washington, DC 20542

Mailing lists are maintained for the cited series (i.e., *Added Entries*, Reference Circulars, Reference Bibliographies, and the NLS directory, *Library Resources for the Blind and Physically Handicapped*) and are available only for libraries or organizations. The lists are maintained under the name of each library or organization. We will add a second line to identify an office or individual if needed, as requested. *Added Entries*, the quarterly listing of items added to the NLS Reference Section collections, highlights *all* new NLS publications. Libraries may want to be placed on the *Added Entries* mailing list only, and then request single copies of new items as they are announced there.

## REFERENCES

Rosen, Leslie, "Online Resources in Blindness and Disability: An International Overview," *Journal of Visual Impairment and Blindness*, March 1989: 156-159.

Library of Congress. National Library Service for the Blind and Physically Handicapped. *That All May Read: Library Service for Blind and Physically Handicapped People*. Washington: 1983. 517p. Free.

# III. SERVICE WITHIN AND WITHOUT THE LIBRARY

## Servicing the Various Publics at a State Supported Academic Library

Mary E. Boulanger

**SUMMARY.** Reference librarians and administrators are always concerned about ways to provide the best service to their patrons. The traditional user groups of the academic library are the faculty, staff, and students of the college or university. In a publicly supported academic library, patrons come from the general community, including children, adolescents, and business people, as well as from the university. This article emphasizes the importance of examining the reference service currently provided, recognizing and identifying the needs of various user groups both within and outside the university community, recognizing current budgetary and staff limitations at the library, and setting priorities for future service opportunities.

### INTRODUCTION

Service is a word or idea often spoken of in the library literature, both theoretically and practically. It is, after all, a major component

Mary E. Boulanger is Reference Librarian at the University of Wisconsin-Milwaukee Golda Meir Library, P.O. Box 604, Milwaukee, WI 53201.

*103*

of what libraries and librarians are about. Whether it is being evaluated, standardized, expanded, cut back, improved, eroded, or something else, it is a topic of interest especially to those on the "front lines" or public service positions. There is even talk of a philosophy of service, and service values, that theoretically should be part of every reference librarian's code of behavior.[1] What is not always mentioned, is that the resources of the library, including service, can be put under increasing strain by user groups who are not specifically mentioned within the library's mission statement. This is especially true in the state supported academic library, which opens its doors to the community at large as well as to students, faculty and staff. Library administrations may have to make hard decisions on what level of service to provide to various groups, considering their needs and the finite resources of the library.

At this point, some people might argue that different levels of service mean an elitist philosophy of service. On the contrary, it is a realistic acknowledgement that though we are trying to serve as many needs as budget and staff allow, the academic library can not be all things to all people. For example, our library is situated next door to an elementary school. Some of the young students occasionally wander into the reference room and ask for help in finding material to do their homework. We assist them whenever possible. However, an academic library will rarely be able to provide the kinds of activities, material, and service to children that a school media center, or the children's section of the local public library can provide. In the course of this article, we will examine the diverse groups that make up our clientele, will look at the challenges involved for each group.

## BACKGROUND

The University of Wisconsin-Milwaukee campus is located in a residential neighborhood ten minutes from downtown Milwaukee. The Golda Meir Library is one of three large research libraries in the city of Milwaukee, with Marquette University Memorial Library and the Milwaukee Public Central Library being the others. UW-Milwaukee is one of only two institutions granting doctoral degrees in the University of Wisconsin System. It is an urban university with an enrollment of approximately 25,000, drawing students and faculty not only from southeastern Wisconsin, but from across the United States and 97 countries around the world. It is one of the largest universities to have one centralized library, which contains over three million catalogued items. Our student body and faculty are diverse in age, sex, race, ethnic background, marital status and in most other demographic characteristics.

The reference department is small for a university of its size. There are six reference librarians whose primary duties include staffing the reference desk, and the department administrator, interlibrary loan librarian and data base services librarian, who help out at the desk when necessary. A librarian from the circulation department also works the reference desk a few hours a week. Two of the librarians are on ten month appointments; three are on eleven month appointments. One of the librarians is also the government documents librarian. The six librarians, with help from the ILL and DBS librarians, are responsible for staffing the reference desk 82 hours a week while school is in session. The microforms area is also part of the reference department.

## TRADITIONAL CLIENTELE: FACULTY

> In their lives, time is one of their most precious commodities, and they are impatient and frustrated to learn that the library reference desk is not a McDonalds's service counter where quick stops yield fast information in neat, take-out containers.[2]

While Wagner and Kappner are writing about non-traditional students, their words could apply to many of our "traditional" students, and some faculty as well. The faculty and staff are heavy users of the library, as measured by circulation statistics. The reference staff interacts on a daily basis with many of them. Since faculty and academic staff tend to be among the more sophisticated users of the library, the questions they ask of the reference staff can be more esoteric and/or complex. They also are usually more able, though not necessarily more willing, to figure out how to use various reference sources on their own once a librarian gets them started.

The faculty are heavy users of the Data Base Services, requesting 20-30 per cent of the computer searches performed each year. As an aid to the research and publishing role of the faculty, the online literature search has proven a tremendous time saver in the quest for materials on the researcher's topic. At the same time, the librarian who works with faculty for a data base search gets a more in-depth understanding of someone's topic of interest or research than is possible in an interview at the reference desk. Though we would like to do more, with our small reference staff we are unlikely to take on a more "proactive" role in supporting faculty research, as is suggested by some in the literature.[3] Nor is it likely that activities such as becoming intimately acquainted with the area of research and the research process of individual researchers, will become common among academic librarians without reallocation of staff and cutbacks in other reference services.

There is wide variation of opinion among the faculty concerning the library's function in support of the teaching role of the faculty and the education process. It is not necessarily bad to have different views, but it seems to indicate a need for better communication between library staff and faculty. Several authors have written on this issue.[4,5,6] One of the problems typical to this gap in understanding is the assignment of the same topic for everyone in the class to write about. While a large research library is expected to tailor its collection development to the needs of the teaching and research taking place there, there are still only going to be so many books on the current "hot topics" such as drug testing, the greenhouse effect, or Virginia Woolf, in the library. Much of the students' frustration is avoided when they may choose among several different research topics, and they are also more likely to learn the library skills needed in future coursework. The reference staff has started a project to work with faculty and teaching assistants as they devise library assignments for their classes. Deborah Fink has written an excellent list of "do's and don'ts" for this kind of assignment.[7]

## UNIVERSITY STUDENTS

The average age of the students at UWM is 25.5 years. Many of them could be classified as "non-traditional," have full or part time jobs, families to support, come from a minority group, or some combination of the above. The university offers a large number of evening courses to handle the large demand. At the library, the reference department schedules a professional librarian at the desk until 10:00 PM most week nights while school is in session, and aims many of its special services at the undergraduate and graduate students.

Bibliographic instruction is provided in the day and evening at the request of faculty and teaching assistants for individual classes. Over 2600 UWM students attended 114 library orientations or other forms of bibliographic instruction during the last academic year. Faculty and teaching assistants usually call to arrange the vast majority of these sessions with a few originating at a librarian's suggestion. All the regular reference staff provides this type of instruction. One of the reference librarians has been designated the bibliographic instruction coordinator, whose job is to assign orientations to specific librarians, usually based on subject expertise and schedule considerations. When the orientation is set up, the librarian will request a copy of any assignment the class will be doing in the library. If there is anything problematic about it, the teacher can be contacted and/or the reference staff warned about the situation.

Other services include tours of the library, arranged by the BI coordinator, which are offered the second week of each semester, and are attended almost exclusively by students. Undergraduates and graduate students have interlibrary loan privileges and many use Data Base Services as well, requesting 50 and 20 per cent of all data base searches, respectively. The most heavily used, or "popular" indexes are shelved on special index tables in direct line of sight of the reference desk.

There is, of course, more that can be done for students. Several studies have indicated that barriers exist, both psychological and physical, to effective service to academic library patrons,[8,9,10] Several years ago the reference staff received a few comments on how intensely we seemed to be buried in our work at the reference desk, and people didn't want to bother us. A sign was made and placed on the reference desk saying, "PLEASE INTERRUPT," in an attempt to ease some of the apprehension with which some folks approach a librarian. It is a rare hour on the desk when a patron doesn't comment about the sign and offer to interrupt.

## *LIBRARY AND INFORMATION SCIENCE STUDENTS*

At UW-Milwaukee there is a distinct subdivision of graduate students which place unique demands upon reference resources, and create unique opportunities as well. These are the students in the School of Library and Information Science. Though they are relatively few in number their impact is high, especially when they are assigned to examine basic reference sources. In earlier times when the reference department was able to order multiple copies of the heavily used reference tools, the library school students usually had no problem finding copies of *Ulrich's Periodicals Directory* or the *American Library Directory*, for example, that they could study. Now, the one and only copy of these items is located behind the reference desk, and have to be asked for. The SLIS students ask for other reference sources that *aren't* behind the desk as well because they can't find them on the reference shelves (usually because someone in their class is using them). Fortunately, the missing items will usually turn up within a week or so, though not always on time for a particular assignment.

The presence of students who plan to become librarians or other information professionals creates positives for the library as well. Though many of the SLIS students are already working in a library or elsewhere, others seek opportunities to gain valuable experience by working at the university library. In addition to the usual work-study positions to be found there, the library has an intern program in conjunction with SLIS to provide meaningful professional experience for those enrolled in it. There are currently interns in the reference area, technical services and the American Geographical Society Collection at the library. The reference department intern, after a period of training by the department administrator, spends all of their working hours (16-20 hours a week) at the reference desk working with a reference librarian. Towards the end of the year they spend in the department, they have the opportunity to work alone at the desk, and attend departmental meetings and workshops. Both library staff and SLIS students have found the intern program to be a mutually beneficial experience.

## FOREIGN AND DISABLED STUDENTS

Another body of students which presents unique service challenges is the international or foreign student. UW-Milwaukee currently has 744, or three per cent of its students hailing from other countries. Many have only a rudimentary knowledge of the English language, and have only a vague idea of how an academic library works in the United States. Part of the problem may lie in the vast differences that exist in the student's experience of libraries in their homeland.[11,12] The problem is made worse by a heavy concentration of foreign students in the sciences and engineering. It has happened on occasion that a librarian would ask a patron to write down a request, after hearing it without comprehending, only to find that they still could not understand what the patron needed.

The university itself provides an orientation which includes the library, that all new foreign students are invited, though not required, to attend. The reference staff has become more sensitive to the cultural differences of foreign students, especially ones from the Middle East and East Asia, but more can be done. The presence of a bilingual reference librarian, has helped greatly in dealing with Spanish speaking students and faculty, both foreign and American-born. Much has been written recently on ways to increase understanding and communicate more effectively with foreign students,[13,14] and ways to improve their understanding of the role of the library.[15,16]

One small but important group of students are the disabled students. These include visually, hearing, and motor impaired individuals. Accessibility, communication, and unfortunately, negative attitudes towards the disabled, can be problems at some university libraries.[17,18] At UW-Milwaukee there is an Office for Disabled Students which provides counseling and other services to their clientele. The library circulation desk has policies for assisting students with disabilities in retrieving materials from the library stacks. The recent library expansion and remodelling included the addition of a more accessible elevator, and the removal of steps at the entrances to the library. (Doors that open automatically already were in place.) New and larger signage has also been installed. All sections of the library stacks are now accessible to wheelchair-bound patrons. The reference policy and practice is to extend whatever assistance is necessary to disabled patrons, to facilitate the use of reference service and resources.

## NON-UNIVERSITY CLIENTELE

In these times of fiscal austerity, each library makes hard decisions about which groups they are able to serve and which not. Because UW-Milwaukee is a state-supported institution, the library cannot turn away potential patrons who do not belong to the university community. Anyone who wishes to make use of the library and its materials may do so on the premises. Circulation policy is more limited, but persons may join the Friends of the Library group for $25.00 and apply for a special permit to check out materials. Except for Interlibrary Loan and Data Base Services, there is no distinction between UWM and non-UWM users when it comes to reference services.

Most of the public and academic libraries and many of the special libraries in the greater Milwaukee area belong to LCOMM, the Library Consortium of Metropolitan Milwaukee. One of its primary activities is the Infopass system, through which library patrons may borrow materials from other libraries in the system when the originating library does not own the requested material. The UWM library does a high amount of traffic in Infopasses, both lending and borrowing, and the system usually works very well. During 1988, 113 were issued by reference staff to UWM students, and 402 were issued by other libraries for their patrons to use here. Most people like the time saved by retrieving the material themselves versus traditional interlibrary loan service.

Students from other colleges in the area use our library often, especially during breaks or between class sessions on their campus. Students from other UW-System universities are a much smaller group of users, but especially noticeable when our students are away. These "extra" students pose few problems for reference staff, except when sheer numbers keep us from serving our own students and faculty. The ones who attend school locally are covered by the Infopass system, if they wish to check out any books. All students of the UW-System campuses are eligible to receive a special borrower's permit, if they request it.

## GENERAL COMMUNITY

As a rule, large university libraries do not have to be concerned with serving their local communities, because these communities are usually large enough to require and support public libraries to fulfill their information needs.[19]

Though this may be the case in Canada, at UW-Milwaukee we do have to be concerned with the information needs of the surrounding communities, since their residents ask us to be. As was mentioned earlier in the article, the Milwaukee Public Library is one of the premier research libraries in the state. MPL and more than thirty branches of the Milwaukee County Federated Library System serve the city and nearby suburbs well. However, the UW-Milwaukee campus is located in a residential area, near the north shore suburbs. Next door to the library is an elementary school, and a few blocks away is Riverside University High School, with which the university has a special relationship. For many of the local residents, many of whom are students and faculty, our library is more convenient, if not physically closer than the nearest public library. Consequently, we receive many requests at the reference desk of a "public library" nature.

Several years ago, after much heated debate, the reference staff decided that since we could not easily tell who was asking these questions (our primary user groups or not), or even if there were academic or scholarly bases for the questions or not, we were obliged to answer them within the limits of our collection and expertise. Someone asking about the participants of the 1957 World Series was most likely not writing a term paper or scholarly article on baseball, for example, but the possibility was there, as would be a convenient source of information at the reference desk, the latest *World Almanac*. Someone needing a 1972 Dodge Dart car manual or an easy recipe for German chocolate cake, on the other hand, would be politely referred to the public library, since we have very few cook books in the collection and no car manuals.

There are some special collections at the Golda Meir Library that attract extra use from the community and beyond. Two that deserve mention are the American Geographical Society Collection and the microfilm collection of 19th century birth, death, and marriage records of Wisconsin counties. The AGS Collection came to the university in 1979 from New York and is a vast storehouse of maps, atlases, photographs, and books and other materials relating to almost any geographical and some geological topics. Rare maps from the 16th century and LANDSAT satellite images from the space age are only some of the treasures held in the collection. The AGSC staff also produce *Current Geographical Publications*, an index of periodicals relating to the various aspects of geography.

The Church of Jesus Christ of Latter Day Saints has long been interested in genealogy for religious reasons. Through the auspices of the Genealogical Society of Utah they produced microfilm copies of county birth, death, marriage, probate, name change, and other records from across the country, and donated them to various state historical societies. The State Historical Society of Wisconsin set was deposited at the Area Research Center located here in the Golda Meir Library at UW-Milwaukee. These records have since been augmented by other county records, and are extremely popular with local historians and genealogy buffs.

## BUSINESS COMMUNITY

The most visible way the library serves the business community is through Data Base Services, which provides bibliographic printouts for a fee to the university community as well as to people in business. The charges to faculty, staff, students and to those working for a nonprofit institution are based solely on the direct costs of the online search. On searches for those in the business community, however, the state of Wisconsin requires the library to add a surcharge to the cost, to prevent any unfair competition with independent online search services in the area.

Legal personnel, especially those working in smaller law firms in the area, visit the reference legal collection often. Though

UW-Milwaukee does not have a law school, the library houses many legal reference sources, including legal encyclopedias, reporting services for the United States Supreme Court and all regional reporting services, and both federal and Wisconsin laws, statutes, and regulations. A special collection of tax materials, including tax court proceedings, IRS regulations, and other tax reporting services is located in the library as well. One of the reference librarians has responsibility for this subject area, and is frequently consulted by her colleages when legal or tax questions arise at the reference desk.

Information brokers are relatively rare in the Milwaukee area, but there are at least two who use the Golda Meir Library on a regular basis. The literature is full of references to problems or potential conflicts of interest in allowing information brokers to use a particular library or service.[20] We have not had many difficulties with brokers at the library. Perhaps because one of the brokers formerly was employed by the library, and another has taught a course for the School of Library and Information Science on campus, the relationship has been cordial. There are no areas, with the possible exception of Data Base Services, where the library is in direct competition for services or resources with information brokers.

## CHILDREN AND ADOLESCENTS

Adults are not the only members of the community who use the academic library. The Golda Meir Library has a special relationship with some of our younger users. As was mentioned earlier in the article, students from the elementary school next door and other youngsters come to the library for help with their homework, to find a good book to read, or just to wait for their parents who are studying/researching/checking out books at the library. Sometimes the parent(s) come along too, asking the questions their child is too shy or embarrassed to ask. These young users very rarely cause any disturbance, nor do we appear to have any "latch-key" children. (There are some skateboarders who sometimes frequent the mall outside the library, but they are primarily high school age and older.) The main problem comes when trying to explain to a child or their parent that we are not likely to have the right kind of books for their science fair or social studies project. The Curriculum Collection of the library, which has materials of grade level K-12 for students in education and teachers to consult is sometimes referred to in this kind of situation. However, it was never meant to be a "children's room." Another library with a similar situation, the Arizona State University-West Campus, has been written up in an interesting account by Carol Burroughs Hammond.[21]

The Golda Meir Library has developed a unique relationship with a city elementary school that shares the same name: the Golda Meir School. This is a specialty school in the Milwaukee Independent School District for gifted and talented children in grades three through five. Several times a year groups of fourth and fifth graders come to the library and attend hands on sessions at the library's online catalog, the microforms area, and the American Geographical Society Collection. At each area one or two library staff help the students complete part of their library "assignment" by demonstrating how to use the resources at hand. Several weeks prior to the students' arrival, one of the reference librarians who also serves as outreach coordinator for the library, discusses with their teachers possible topics for the Golda Meir children to work on when they come to the library. After a brief welcoming talk and orientation, the children are divided into three groups, spend approximately 25 minutes in each area, then rotate to the next area. It is seen by both teachers and students as a valuable and informative introduction to the university and its library. Though the students are a bit young to be thinking much about college, the outing provides a positive experience of UW-Milwaukee which they may remember several years down the road.

Like many other academic libraries, we work with high school groups in the area in an effort to foster community relations and as an aid to recruitment.[22,23,24] High school teachers will call to arrange a library tour or orientation for their group. Sometimes they will have a paper or other assignment to work on at the library. In other cases the students are just coming to get an overview of how a college library differs from what they are used to in their school. This is a very popular program, so much so that we have to limit the size of the groups and the number each semester. The outreach coordinator usually works with the groups when they arrive, giving them a brief overview usually followed by a tour. Sometimes the high school students are "turned loose" in the library to work on their projects. It is difficult to distinguish some of these users from college undergraduates. This can create problems when a reference librarian inadvertently refers someone to the circulation desk who might not be permitted to check out materials.

In addition to the regular high school tours, the university has a special relationship with a nearby high school: Riverside University High School. Some of the classes taught there can be transferred as college credit at UW-Milwaukee. RHS students come frequently to our library, especially those working in college level courses, and can arrange to check out materials with a special permit.

## OUTLOOK FOR FUTURE REFERENCE SERVICES: QUALITY VS. QUANTITY

Library literature in recent times has been full of new reference services and new ways to provide old ones, even including how to keep up the morale of the reference staff in the wake of the new wave of services.[25] Unfortunately, before a library can enthusiastically embrace an expansion of the reference ideal, serious evaluation needs to take place, evaluation of current reference service and policies. Deciding what is essential, and what is not, is imperative unless there is unlimited funding for these services. It will be easier for both library administration and reference departments to make these decisions, if priorities for services and their target groups have been worked out ahead of time.

How does one evaluate needs and priorities? It helps if there is a mission statement or at least a policy manual for the library and the reference department. For the academic library, the mission of the college or university should also be kept in mind. The reference department at UW-Milwaukee has a policy manual that is invaluable as a record of what services we provide and to whom.[26] Policies do change over time and a policy manual loses value if it is not updated or revised periodically. Though it can not guarantee total consistency in service, it serves as an ideal and standard to which the reference staff can refer. As new needs are recognized, some practices can be examined and changes noted in the manual.

Reference librarians, according to Bunge, may have the best job in the library,[27] but they need to educate people that good reference service isn't just done with mirrors, a good pair of shoes and a smile. The reference staff try to maintain a delicate balance between providing needed information and educating patrons in the ways of obtaining the information themselves. Since library administrators are usually reluctant to reduce service, and sometimes request that their staff find ways to provide even more service with the same budget, it is imperative that reference librarians develop a sense of their own limitations. Perhaps there is room for increased productivity or efficiency among the staff. On the other hand, however, the reference staff may already be stretched to its capacity, and library administration needs to be made aware of this before new services are proposed.

Lou Holtz, the college football coach once said that when he died he wanted the inscription, "I told you I was sick," put on his tombstone. Reference service has been around for almost a century,[28] and few are predicting its imminent demise. But as budgets get tighter, colleges and universities compete for fewer students, and technology fills more and more roles in libraries, a little preventive medicine, or self examination seems to be in order to ensure that the primary goal of reference service at an academic library, unlocking the library's resources for the academic community, is fulfilled.

## REFERENCES

1. Finks, Lee W. "Values without Shame." *American Libraries* 20(4):352-354. April 1989.

2. Wagner, Collette A. and Augusta S. Kappner. "The Academic Library and the Non-Traditional Student." in *Libraries and Search for Academic Excellence*, eds., Breivik, Patricia Senn and Robert Wedgeworth. Metuchen, N.J.: Scarecrow. 1988.

3. Grover, Robert and Martha L. Hale. "The Role of the Librarian in Faculty Research." *College and Research Libraries* 49(1):9-15. January 1988.

4. Commerton, B. Anne. "Building Faculty/Library Relationships: Forging the Bond." *The Bookmark* 45:17-20. Fall 1986

5. Somerville, Arleen N. Somerville. "Information Services to the Academic Scientific Community in the 1980s." *Reference Librarian* no.16:125-139. Winter 1986.

6. Miller, Richard E. "The Tradition of Reference Service in the Liberal Arts College Library." *RQ* 25(4):461-467. Summer 1986.

7. Fink, Deborah. "What You Ask for Is What You Get: Some Do's and Don'ts for Assigning Research Projects." *Research Strategies* 4:91-93. Spring 1986.

8. Dequin, Henry C., Irene Schilling, and Samuel Huang. "The Attitudes of Academic Librarians toward Disabled Persons." *Journal of Academic Librarianship* 14(1):28-31. March 1988.

9. Hatchard, Desmond B. and Phyllis Toy. "The Psychological Barriers Between Library Users and Library Staff." *Australian Academic & Research Libraries* 17:63-69. June 1986.

10. Durfee, Linda J. "Student Awareness of Reference Services in a Liberal Arts College Library." *Library Quarterly* 56(3):286-302. 1986.

11. Sarkodi-Mensah, Kwasi. "In the Words of a Foreigner." *Research Strategies* 4:30-31. Winter 1986.

12. Macdonald, Gina and Elizabeth Sarkodi-Mensah. "ESL Students and American Libraries." *College and Research Libraries* 49(5):425-431. September 1988.

13. Greenfield, Louise, Susan Johnston, and Karen Williams. "Educating the World: Training Library Staff to Communicate Effectively with International Students." Journal of Academic Librarianship 12(4):227-231. 1986.

14. Ball, Mary Alice and Molly Mahony. "Foreign Students, Libraries, and Culture." College and Research Libraries 48(2):160-166. March 1987.

15. Moorhead, Wendy. "Ignorance was our Excuse." *College & Research Libraries News* 47(9):585-587. October 1986.

16. Aman, Mohammed and Mary Jo Aman. "Reference Services and Global Awareness." *Reference Librarian* no. 17:45-50. Spring 1987.

17. Broadway, Marsha D. and Sharon W. Self. "Disabled Students in an Academic Library: A Survey." *Southeastern Librarian* 36:84-87. Winter 1986.

18. Mularski, Carol. "Academic Library Service to Deaf Students: Survey and Recommendations." *RQ* 26(4):477-486. Summer 1987.

19. Savage, D. A. "Town and Gown Re-examined: the Role of the Small University Library in the Community." *Canadian Library Journal* 45:291-295. October 1988.

20. Kinder, Robin and Bill Katz, eds.. Information Brokers and Reference Services. New York, NY: Haworth Press, Inc. 1988. (also published as *The Reference Librarian* no. 22, 1988.)

21. Hammond, Carol Burroughs. "Kids, the Academic Library, and the Schools." *College & Research Library News* 50(4):264-266. April 1989.

22. Thompson, Ronelle K. H. and Glenda T. Rhodes. "Recruitment: A Role for the Academic Library?" *College & Research Library News* 47(9):575-577. October 1986.

23. Miller, Rosalind and Ralph Russell. "High School Students and the College Library: Problems and Possibilities." *Southeastern Librarian* 37:36-40. Summer 1987.

24. LeClercq, Angie. "The Academic Library/High School Library Connection: Needs Assessment and Proposed Model." *Journal of Academic Librarianship* 12(1):12-18. March 1986.

25. There are too many good articles to mention individually, but services such as Information & Referral, term paper consultations, and online catalog training are heavily written about.

26. The University of Wisconsin-Milwaukee Golda Meir Library. *Reference Manual*. Milwaukee, WI: UWM Golda Meir Library. November 1984.

27. Bunge, Charles A. "Potential and Reality at the Reference Desk: Reflections on a 'Return to the Field.'" *Journal of Academic Librarianship* 10(3):128-133. July 1984.

28. Ford, Barbara J. "The Future of Reference Service – Reference Service: Past, Present, and Future." *College & Research Library News* 49(9):578-582. October 1988.

# Nonusers of Academic Libraries:
# Academic Lifestyles
# and Reference Services

Patricia A. Cannon

**SUMMARY.** This essay proposes the identification and study of nonusers of academic library reference services. Using the techniques previously applied to different classes of public library users, researchers could benefit from information already available, as well as undertake survey research on lifestyles in academe. The discussion puts forth the claim that nonusers of academic libraries are potential users belonging to the same three groups as current users: faculty, staff, and students. A brief overview of the results of the application of lifestyles research to public library user groups is provided. Finally, the article describes some lifestyle characteristics of each of the three groups and their possible implications for academic library reference services.

## INTRODUCTION

Academic and public libraries share a proclivity toward the user study. Anyone with sufficient need or interest to come in the door is, by definition a user, a subject worthy of study. That the user is readily accessible further encourages taking advantage of this dependable source. But a related area of inquiry, the identification of nonusers, has received relatively sparse attention in academic libraries. Why? The answer may lie in the nature of the academic library itself. Public libraries often set out to serve entire communities. An academic library, on the other hand, focuses on the members of a community directly affiliated with its academic institution.

---

Patricia A. Cannon is Assistant Professor, Department of Library & Information Studies, Northern Illinois University, DeKalb, IL 60115-2854.

The nonusers of an academic library's services, therefore, belong to the same categories as its users: faculty, staff, and students. Perhaps it is assumed that all three categories of users are already targeted and that any members of either group not attracted by current marketing strategies are unreachable. This assumption would make attempts to identify and study nonusers of academic libraries a moot point, at best.

Sometimes, however, a line of thinking not considered applicable to a situation can provide valuable insights. What if academic library nonusers, specifically those not availing themselves of reference services, were studied using a lifestyles approach, such as has been applied in the public library setting? What would be the probable methods and findings, and their implications for reference service?

For purposes of these observations, reference work will be defined as encompassing both reference services and the collection, notably but not exclusively reference materials. A preliminary examination requires a broad perspective that touches, if only superficially, on a number of topics. Important related topics include user/nonuser dichotomies, cost/benefit considerations from the point of view of the user, typical academic lifestyles of the three groups, and reference services to be offered.

## USERS AND NONUSERS OF PUBLIC LIBRARIES

Since the early 1970's, extensive reader surveys conducted by both private and public organizations have assisted public libraries in serving their communities.[1] Employing the customary definition of a user as a person who uses the library at least once a year,[2] the surveys place respondents in user/nonuser categories based upon their answers to one or more questions regarding frequency of library visits, telephone calls, etc. The findings of these surveys have identified traits of those who do and do not use public libraries. According to several of these studies, the traits associated with library use include: avid reading, educational achievement, wide-ranging interests, and active participation in civic, cultural, and political activities.[3]

In addition to identifying user traits, the data have been used to distinguish between two subgroups of nonusers: potential users and hard-core nonusers.[4] The labels mean what they imply. Hard-core nonusers are those deemed unlikely, due to established life patterns of inactivity, to be attracted to libraries. Potential users resemble users in their active lifestyles and can presumably be drawn to use library services.

According to Braunstein, the key to attracting people to the library is a combination of minimizing their costs and maximizing benefits.[5] He suggested that the user invests time, money, and effort in a trip to the library; these costs are weighed in the patron's mind against the probability of obtaining the item sought (with both bibliographic and textual access considered). D'Elia, in a telephone survey conducted for a branch of the Saint Paul Public Library, concluded that potential users attributed their failure to actually use library services to inconvenience.[6] The major inconveniences named were library hours and the perceived difficulty of returning materials by their due dates. The chief complaint was of library inaccessibility, the equivalent of the cost factors of time and effort. In attempting to reach nonusers, libraries have two primary marketing strategies open to them: User Group Expansion, extending present services to nonusers; and Diversification, developing new services for them.[7]

## NONUSERS OF ACADEMIC LIBRARY REFERENCE SERVICES

Some of the findings already noted might be applied to users of academic libraries. If the arbitrarily-chosen, once-a-year standard previously cited qualifies one as an academic library user, and if academic library use is also associated with the educational, motivational, and active lifestyle traits attributed to public library users, it appears probable that the majority of nonusers of academic libraries belong to the subgroup of potential users. Assuming this to be the case, any efforts toward identifying nonusers would be cause for optimism about increasing the academic library's user base. Identifying nonusers would involve taking a closer look at the three groups an academic library expects to attract.

Results of a telephone survey of 22 academic libraries' reference departments suggest that those who visit or telephone a reference department receive equal or nearly equal treatment, regardless of their status.[8] In attempting to answer his research question of whether "academic library reference services [are] essentially egalitarian or elitist,"[9] Berry questioned reference department heads about library reference staff responses to different user types. He asked about affiliation or status as prior conditions for responding to reference questions, loan periods for circulating materials, additional services provided to specific groups, and time spent. Essentially, he found reference departments committed to offering the same quality, time, and level of service, whatever the user's status (which is often not identified by or apparent to the reference librarian). Some notable exceptions to this general rule were the usual longer loan periods for faculty and graduate students, and limits or restrictions on interlibrary loan requests placed for undergraduates. The one group experiencing discrimination in obtaining reference services was not among the three already mentioned. It is that group of users discovered to be unaffiliated with the academic institution where services are sought. This distinction in willingness to provide services was more frequently mentioned by libraries of private than public academic institutions.

If libraries are to identify and attract those potential users who are at present nonusers, the even-handed approach reference librarians espouse is encouraging. Although there is always room for improvement, at least all three groups seem likely to benefit from additional efforts at reaching nonusers. Because many academic libraries maintain a schedule of longer hours than do public libraries, surveys of potential academic library users might not be expected to pinpoint this as an inconvenience, but might instead protest the limited availability of reference assistance during those longer hours. The problem of inconvenient due dates might exist in academic libraries as well as public, particularly among undergraduate students and staff, and should not be overlooked as a factor in the use of reference services.

One approach to locating nonusers of a specific college library is to compile a campus-wide checklist of all groups of potential users in each of the three broad categories (faculty, staff, and students). The list could then be compared to library policies and procedures, especially those in the areas of reference services and collection development, to see whether each group is individually identified or directly incorporated into a broader, obviously applicable category of people to be served. Examples of divisions to list are: for faculty, academic departments and colleges or schools; for staff, each separately identified unit (i.e., student personnel services, security, continuing education, etc.); for students, undergraduates, extension, etc. Categories of academic workers left out of library plans and policies or given merely superficial attention might be expected to contain some of the library's nonusers.

Use studies may or may not be of assistance in their flip side: who does not use or makes inadequate use of a library's services. Without some direct questioning of users to provide additional information, traditional usage statistics are of little value.[10] The heavier a library's emphasis on research activities, the less important overall library statistics will be for assessing reference effectiveness. Reference users themselves are hard to identify. Even if a concerted effort is made to contact each person calling or visiting the reference department, there are the continuing problems of staffing the data collection effort, choosing representative times to collect data, and finding a way to include users who send a surrogate (e.g., a research assistant). A related problem is that of gathering reference statistics, often inaccurate because they are assigned a low priority among reference librarians due to the perception they are impracticable.[11]

## *FACULTY LIFESTYLES*

In the literature on academic libraries, user studies predominate, due perhaps to the accessibility of freshmen attending library tours. Little is said about nonusers. Yet, as Lowell Martin commented, "The case can be advanced that if any formal study is to be made . . . it would best be directed to those who do not come to the library," in part because "general library use studies . . . tell us what is rather than what should be."[12]

It is my contention that the nonusers of academic libraries, most of whom are potential users, exist among each of the three dominant groups to be found on any campus: faculty, staff, and students.

The professional literature of both librarians and the various academic support services occupations implies that two of the three groups, those most readily identified with an academic institution's teaching function, receive nearly all the attention. One of those groups is faculty.

The accepted mode of association among teaching faculty is one of collegiality. Collegiality is the natural result of the tradition of academic freedom and its application in the form of policies such as tenure. In an article on collection development in academic libraries, Thomas noted that academic institutions tend to operate according to two distinct systems: the laisses-faire collegial approach applied to faculty, and the more authoritarian hierarchy to which campus support services must adhere.[13]

A recent complaint issuing from teaching faculty at campuses nationwide concerns a new generation of administrators who, according to Bilik and Blum, threaten to "drag higher education into the corporate past,"[14] by relying on outmoded management concepts already rejected by some of the country's top corporations. Ironically, it was scholarly research on college campuses that affirmed the value of the spirit of collegiality to corporations, which are now adopting that system, while the researchers' own campus administrators reject the tradition. Libraries house, organize, and disseminate the research that could better inform decision-makers about these issues. What are librarians doing, or should they be doing, to address this particular informational need of both faculty and administration?

Faculty are granted tenure and promotions, their individual assurances of academic freedom, on the basis of their performance of activities related to three roles: teaching, service to professional associations and the public, and research and publication.[15] Both research and teaching roles practically necessitate their use, to one degree or another, of libraries. Are there nonusers who are faculty? Possibly so. From the librarian's perspective, it may be obvious that a personal library cannot be sufficiently inclusive or broad in scope to meet all of even one faculty member's needs. To the college professor with a narrow teaching specialization and research interests, it may be less so. Nonetheless, teaching faculty, regardless of discipline, are in one way or another some of the heaviest and most consistent users of reference services.

## STUDENT LIFESTYLES

The other group associated with the teaching function, and thus receiving significant attention, is students. With bibliographic instruction common in academic library settings, it is doubtful that students who enter campus as freshmen will be nonusers. But some freshmen may visit the library only when forced to do so, and attrition statistics may be evidence of this. While a number of studies have focused on possible causes of student attrition, and these often mention the importance of strong study skills and habits, they seldom mention the library specifically, unless appearing in professional library literature. Other professional groups appear to leave the library out when framing their survey questions. For example Bean's model for student retention decisions weighs academic integration heavily as a factor.[16] His definition of academic integration includes such elements as study skills, relationships with faculty, class attendance, and certainty about majors.

In a recent survey, Rotter applied that model to the development of a questionnaire administered to 59% of all freshmen students at New Jersey Institute of Technology. If libraries were anywhere noted in the survey instrument, this is not apparent in the article. Yet, judging by her findings that dropouts spent less time physically on campus, less time studying while on campus, and less time on academic matters than other students, the library seems to be at the very least peripherally involved in student success or attrition. One mention of note was that "those who are at risk [for dropping out] spend more time in the cafeteria than those who are not."[17] Might it be logical to assume that those who are not, who spend more time on their academic careers, spend more time in the library? This is not clear from this and similar articles.

Student populations in the United States today are more diverse than ever before in several key respects: academic preparation, vocational background, age, socioeconomic status, and motivation to attend college.[18] Perhaps those students most likely to be nonusers are those never exposed to formal library instruction or to instruction for the particular academic library they are now expected to use. The groups involved might include transfer students who may or may not have received help at a two-year college or another institution who now feel intimidated by the size or arrangement of one new to them, graduate students who may be returning to academe after several years' break, and foreign students who may find the classification scheme, layout, and/or procedures new.

Even among that relatively advantaged group of student users, freshmen, some may slip away once their attendance at mandatory sessions expires. For over three-quarters of today's freshmen, an overriding goal in life is to be *very* well off financially.[19] In a keynote address to the National Conference on the Freshman Year Experience, Bradford College President Arthur E. Levine noted that over the past twenty years students' "social and personal commitments continue to decline while job interests rise even further."[20] Only to the extent that these students perceive college, and by implication the library, to be relevant to these life goals can they be expected to return with being forced.

## STAFF LIFESTYLES

The differences between faculty and staff go beyond the different administrative systems applied to the two groups. Library studies which mention any user category other than that of student or faculty sometimes name administrators. When specific job titles of administrators are named, those are invariably upper-level positions, such as president, dean, or provost. Whether other staff are served (although one would assume so) or are even considered an important category of potential users, is not apparent. In other words, the literature on users of academic libraries seems mostly to ignore one potential, even probable, group: the college and university staff in non-teaching positions, both administrative and support positions. Whole realms of the academic work force are ignored: those staff members employed in counseling, placement, student services, continuing education, computer services, and research advisory services, to name only a few.

Not only do librarians leave them out, but writers in these other career fields seem to forget the library when resources are being suggested to colleagues. Considering the tendency not to include this group in library planning or to study their needs in depth, it is little wonder that they fail to perceive the academic library as a valuable resource for day-to-day information on coping with job responsibilities. Reviewing a five-year span of articles in journals devoted to serving these types of groups, journals such as *College Student Journal*, *Guidance and Counseling*, *Journal of College Admissions*, and *Journal of College Placement*, reveals no indication that the library might be useful in developing job skills, learning new techniques or methods, keeping abreast of professional developments, or advancing in one's career. This is true in spite of the fact that the journals obviously cater to professionals working on college and university campuses.

Considering the staff and materials budget cuts many libraries currently face, the marketing strategy of diversification may not be feasible. However, the practice of extending existing services to nonusers holds promise. Part of the current problem might be summarized as a lack of awareness: reference workers' awareness of potential library users at all levels and staff awareness of library materials and services of possible value to them. This is not to suggest that academic libraries should divert their attention from faculty and students to concentrate on this apparently underserved group. Rather, more of an effort might be made to "include them in" when planning and announcing services.

There is one more reason to pay closer attention to these groups. Staff in other non-academic departments may be valuable resource persons for in-house library programming. A well-established liaison with them encourages the development of reciprocal agreements to share ideas, people, and services. Not only might this benefit the library and the staff members, it might enhance the services provided to academic components.

## *CONCLUSION*

The paucity of available information on those not served by academic library reference departments mandates a more concerted effort to study this problem in depth. Research might explore the lifestyles of subgroups within the three broad groups that comprise academe: faculty, staff, and students. A partial solution suggested here is one that might be labeled a type of consciousness-raising, among both librarians and their potential clients. Additional efforts at dealing with the problem could involve the compilation and innovative application of existing data. Lists of people and data previously collected by other campus organizations are a good starting place. Questionnaires could be adapted to serve other types of potential users. A closer inspection of academic library nonusers is both warranted and likely to reap long-term benefits.

## REFERENCES

1. For an overview of three of these, see Art Plotnik, "Naked Came the Reader, or A Tale of Three Surveys," *American Libraries*, 9 (December 1978): 639-640.

2. Douglas L. Zweizig and Brenda Dervin, "Public Library Use, Users, Uses: Advances in Knowledge of the Characteristics and Needs of the Adult Clientele of American Public Libraries," *Advances in Librarianship*, 7 (New York: Academic Press, 1977), 231-255.

3. For example, Michael Madden, "Library User/Nonuser Lifestyles," *American Libraries*, 10 (February 1979): 78-81; George D'Elia, "A Procedure for Identifying and Surveying Potential Users of Public Libraries," *Library Research*, 2 (Fall 1980): 239-249; and W. Theodore Bolton, "Life Style Research: An Aid to Promoting Public Libraries," *Library Journal*, 107 (15 May 1982): 963-968.

4. D'Elia, p. 241.

5. Yale M. Braunstein, "Costs and Benefits of Library Information: The User Point of View," *Library Trends*, 28 (Summer 1979): 79-87.

6. D'Elia, pp. 239-249.

7. H. Igor Ansoff, "Strategies for Diversification," *Harvard Business Review*, 35 (September/October 1957): 113-127.

8. John W. Berry, "Academic Reference Departments and User Groups: A Preliminary Survey," *The Reference Librarian*, 12 (Spring/Summer 1985): 5-16.

9. Berry, p. 6.

10. Mickey Moskowitz, "Collection Development and the College Library: A State-of-the-Art Review," *Collection Building*, 6 (Summer 1984): 5-10.

11. Martin Kesselman and Sarah Barbara Watstein, "The Measurement of Reference and Information Services," *The Journal of Academic Librarianship*, 13 (March 1987): 24-30.

12. Lowell A. Martin, "User Studies and Library Planning," *Library Trends*, 24 (January 1976): 489-490.

13. Lawrence Thomas, "Tradition and Expertise in Academic Library Collec-

tion Development," *College and Research Libraries*, 48 (November 1987): 487-493.

14. Laurie J. Bilik and Mark C. Blum, "Deja Vu All Over Again*: Initiatives in Academic Management," *Academe*, 75 (January/February 1989): 10-13.

15. Peter Seldin, "How Colleges Evaluate Professors," *AAHE Bulletin*, 41 (March 1989): 3-7.

16. John P. Bean, "Assessing and Reducing Attrition," *New Directions for Higher Education*, 14 (1986): 47-61.

17. Naomi G. Rotter, "Student Attrition in a Technological University; Academic Lifestyle," *College Student Journal*, 22 (Fall 1988): 246.

18. Virginia N. Gordon and Thomas J. Grites, "The Freshman Seminar Course: Helping Students Succeed," *Journal of College Student Personnel*, 25 (July 1984): 315-320.

19. Arthur E. Levine, "Hearts and Minds: The Freshman Challenge," *AAHE Bulletin*, 38 (April 1986): 3-6.

20. Levine, p. 4.

# A Critique of the Information Broker: Contexts of Reference Services

## John Buschman

**SUMMARY.** This paper focuses on two basic foundations of reference services: service to people and to book collections. As a critique of the information broker concept, areas of conflict with those foundations are explored. Those conflicts are put in context within the profession and within social trends. The attempt has been to provide a framework for the evidence and thought which contributes to the critique and to provide a much-needed alternative view of information brokerage.

### INTRODUCTION

Reference service in libraries brings with it a background of solid orientation toward people and books. It is the contention of this paper that the background is good and should not be lightly considered. We have seen, and will continue to see, waves of technological change that chip away at older reference orientations and habits. The concept of information broker focuses those changes squarely on the reference librarian and the services offered. I would like to examine characteristics of the context of the information broker and view their effects on traditional reference orientation and services. By relying on an older, and I think good, model of reference service, I want to critique the concept of information broker in order to provide some balance to discussions of our future in library professional literature. Much of the evidence and thought of this critique is contained within library literature. This article is an attempt to identify that evidence and thought which can contribute to a critique

John Buschman is Assistant Professor-Library, Rider College Library, 2083 Lawrenceville Road, Lawrenceville, NJ 08648.

of the concept of information broker and to provide a conceptual framework for that critique.

## TRADITIONAL REFERENCE ORIENTATION

The term traditional is used to describe older reference orientations and it is used consciously. In a prolonged attempt to change a negative (or soft) professional image, librarians have crept away from both the bad and good of our collective past. It is a central idea of this paper that we cannot afford to discard the best of the past or present. As stated in the introduction, traditional reference orientation was toward books and people. Constance Miller and James Rettig cite Samuel Green's 1876 article in *Library Journal* as an early identification of the people/client orientation in reference service. Green's principles, put down upon his successful transformation of the Worcester Free Public Library's reference service, are heavily weighted toward the human side of library inquiry. He sought not only to identify the inquiry, but also to *select* the sources most appropriate. Stress was put on personally showing the patron how to use the books and only eventually teaching them to be more independent.[1]

Sam Walter Foss would express a different approach in 1907 when he stressed the librarian's objectivity in service, yet he retains a basic grounding in service to people: "a librarian is both Greek and Barbarian, Jew and Gentile, realist and romanticist, aristocrat and democrat, theosophist, secularist, orthodox, liberal, populist and patrician. He is all things to all men — and all men are the same to him."[2] This commitment continues through much of what we do today. "Reference encounters with undergraduates often result not only in answering specific questions, but also in personalized instruction in the methods of identifying and retrieving library materials."[3] Our work has yet to grow so abstract as to lose sight of service to people and the human grounding of the entire library process.

Equally clear is the centrality of the book to traditional reference service. It is a tautology to declare the relationship of books to librarianship. The profession would never have existed without the book. Yet the profession, and by definition reference service, has had a special relationship to the book. Arthur Bostwick stated it as "the love of books as a basis for librarianship" and wrote:

> Let us perfect ourselves in all the minutiae of our profession, let us study how to elevate it and make it more effective, but let us not forget the book. . . . Possibly the librarian who reads is lost, but the librarian who has never read, or who, having read, has imbibed from reading no feeling toward books, but those of dislike or indifference, is surely worse than lost — he has, so far as true librarianship goes, never existed.[4]

Contemporary scholars still tend to think of libraries and librarianship in these terms. Oscan Handlin notes that "libraries . . . no longer hold a monopoly on information; a flourishing industry now makes such data available through numerous alternative channels. . . . The library may not be able to compete in this market, and in any case, the effort to do so may divert attention from what it alone can provide — access to its collections. . . ."[5] Perhaps the most eloquent statement of this idea has come from Archibald MacLeish's essay "The Premise of Meaning":

> a library, considered not as a collection of objects that happen to be books but as a number of books that have been chosen to constitute a library, is an extra-ordinary thing. . . . It is not a sort of scholarly filling station where students can repair to get themselves supplied with a tank full of titles; not an academic facility to be judged by the quantity of its resources and the promptness of its service. On the contrary it is an achievement in and of itself . . .[6]

Service to people and books are so much a part of reference, its essence in so many ways, that overlooking them is in some ways effortless. "Progress" in reference service has seen subtle shifts away from these roots. The human side of information retrieval is seen as an area that now needs to be reasserted and watched.[7] Miller and Rettig have identified a significant gap in satisfaction with reference service in the move away from client centered (delivery of information) reference toward teaching information independence.

They see possible obsolescence for reference service in this gap.[8] The library itself is now merely a co-source of information in the way colleges are not marketed. "Library size evolved as a bench-mark by which to judge universities . . . because students wanted access to information. The computer . . . is replacing the library as a 'gateway to information.' "[9]

## *CONTEXT OF THE INFORMATION BROKER*

It can be clearly seen that in new areas of and in demands upon reference, there have been shifts away from traditional reference orientation. These shifts exist in both our self perception and in our public image as well as in the basis of service. The shifts are best captured in the move toward a concept of information broker. I want to next briefly examine this concept and then look at some of its particulars and context. My vantage point has been the funda-mental basis of service to people and books, so critique of informa-tion brokerage will flow from the conflict between the two.

Michael Cart looked for a definition of an information broker and settled on a descriptive quote:

> A very real change in the role of the librarian seems inevitable. As users can make direct use of information online, without the librarian intermediary, a new type of clientele will emerge. Librarians may be much more involved in teaching system search strategies, interpreting information, and helping users decide which online resource to access.[10]

I agree with the choice of description/definition. However, I dis-agree with his contention that this is merely the same old reference librarian dressed up in new clothes. Inherent in this description is a context for reference service (or information brokerage if you pre-fer) that shifts it away from its traditional bases. Indeed, this new context is in some conflict with those bases.

The first of these conflicts is an oft-repeated statement about the relationship of information to books and wisdom. Books are an at-tempt by an author(s) or editor(s) to present and develop an idea or evidence on a topic. The work is meant to stand as a unified unit and contribute to the discourse within its subject. Information is the antithesis of this idea. It is the breaking down of text into smaller, accessible, useful parts regardless of their parent context. Those parts are often unrelated to one another. This is best exemplified by the idea of an accumulation of facts, like a cookbook, and it stands apart from the attempt at structure and coherence in books. As the statement goes, books (and collections of books) are contributors to the wisdom of civilization and information stands as a breakdown of wisdom.[11] While this analysis has probably been flogged too much, it contains within it an essential insight: the breaking down of linear thought of books into bits of information. Currently our capabilities have best tackled periodical and related writings in converting them to information online, but no one seriously doubts that books are the ultimate goal to access online. It is these bits of information which are now an autonomous sphere in their own right and are the basis of the content for the information broker. Pure access to information stands in conflict with service to collections of books.

Privatization of information resources is a well-established trend and can be viewed as another conflict with traditional reference orientation. Perhaps the best known example of this trend is the growing penchant of the federal government to turn information gathered at taxpayers' expense over to private companies to market and sell. A lengthy review is not necessary here since this topic has been well covered in the professional literature.[12] However, there are other areas that are characteristic of privatization of information as well. John Haar raises two crucial points concerning online databases that many libraries *do* provide access to: the company "retains ownership of the databases involved and merely provides temporary and limited access to them" in contrast to the *purchase* of a data base (i.e., an index or an abstract in book form) which provides for public access; *and* access to online databases is necessarily restricted because of cost.[13] We tend to think of these tools as *increasing* information availability, but it is important to note that in their current economic and social contexts, privatized sources of information can block access.

Privatization does not end there. Haar's warning that librarians should not cede control of databases and trust their integrity to their corporate sponsors should not be taken lightly. These are, after all, privately owned resources in a very mutable format and their distribution and content can be political issues as easily as the content of school textbooks. A recent example of this can be seen in the incident of Dun and Bradstreet revoking the password to its database of labor union librarians.[14] Similarly CD-ROM databases will not be the immediate solution either since development and implementation is also in corporate hands and they "are not calculated to maximize the potential of the technology but rather to maintain the profitability of print and online products."[15]

I would also suggest that these developments have led to a privatizing of some book collections. James Govan admirably traces the concept of charging for services back to the introduction of photocopies. Charges for interlibrary loans then took root in several university research libraries and then access charges to visiting scholars were instituted. He notes this as a shift away from service to national scholarship and the public good. Charges for online services are a continuation of this trend. It has reached a point where "some governing boards and administrators . . . are now instructing directors to *produce* income." The result is "a relative indifference to service . . ., often treated cynically and paid mere lip service."[16] He describes this as a "subtle and fundamental change in values and attitudes" which draws much creditability from new approaches to librarianship.

One "rethinking" of the librarian's role seeks to pattern professional conduct after corporate database managers. Librarians it is said, should be responsible for the information they find and give and draw professionalism from vouching for its correctness. Models to be followed are those corporations whose success has been built on service.[17] This seems to be the ultimate form of privatization and a logical step from the production of income and reliance on privatized information. It seems clear that this trend has existed before the present and has extended well beyond the controversies over government information. There have been fundamental changes in approach to both the book and service to people. Access to collections and ideas of public good, once firmly embedded in librarianship, are giving some ground to producing income and consequent turns from service to models of corporate origin. The concept of the information broker is predicated on newer and privatized forms of information, and so it stands within this overall context in conflict with traditional reference bases.

The next step is to look at the nature of the stuff of the information broker: information. The relationship between books and information has been very briefly reviewed, but what one must ask is, what is the context of information and how does that affect reference service? I would suggest that information has been reified and that this has a profound affect on reference service in the context of information brokerage, Reify is defined as "To change a mental attitude or abstraction into a supposed real thing; to attribute objective substantiality to an idea."[18] Theodore Roszak traces the concept of information from the early humdrum of "disjointed matters of fact that came in discrete little bundles" to the megahype of the Information Society. He observes "it is easy to conclude that because we have the ability to transmit more electronic bits more rapidly to more people than ever before, we are making real cultural progress — and that the essence of that progress is information technology."[19] In its rags-to-riches transformation,

> Information has taken on the quality of that impalpable, invisible, but plaudit-winning silk from which the emperor's etherial gown was supposedly spun. The word has received ambitious, global definitions that make it all good things to all people. . . . People who have no clear idea what they mean by information or why they should want so much of it are nonetheless prepared to believe that we live in an Information Age. . . . These often-repeated catchphrases and clichés are the mumbo jumbo of a widespread public cult (and) their very emptiness may allow them to be filled with a mesmerizing glamour.[20]

He and others note that "information . . . is not a discovery but an invention" whose development extends back through industrialization, and its machinery, "the computer, is for the twentieth what the clock was for the seventeenth and eighteenth centuries: the great metaphor under whose sign all things could be gathered."[21] Viewed otherwise, information is "granular" with no inherent grammar, it is *very* perishable, it has little value unto itself only as a reflection of the external world, and it is a consumer commodity. Yet it has attained the status of an objective thing: "it is knowledge reified."[22]

Reification of information has taken hold within the library profession. In some ways "we have permitted technological metaphors . . . and technique itself to so thoroughly pervade out thought processes that we have finally abdicated to technology the very duty to formulate questions."[23] There is some evidence that this is the case. Hernon and McClure note that reference staff have come to depend too much on technology, ignoring (or not knowing of) print equivalents. Reference staff wrongly think of the online catalog as a comprehensive holdings record for their library. They go on to cite other, possible related, reference short-comings as well.[24] James Rice provides a very interesting example as well. He identifies holism and serendipity as two prime virtues of card catalogs. The act of using the card catalog, scanning cards quickly, looking at their cumulative size, age, condition, and the accidental (perhaps subliminal) happening on to good items are all ways that give one a "feel" for the collection, its nature and size. In searching for ways that online catalogs can offset those qualities lost, Rice goes on to *redefine* serendipity and holism into characteristics that will fit an online catalog. Instead of the virtues which are by necessity embedded in the technology of the card catalog, holism and serendipity are now "flexibility," "retrieving relevant citations," and "filtering out noise."[25]

Our literature contains wondrous descriptions of future "books" on hypertext (with the appropriate new technology): "Wouldn't you really love to have a book you could read at the beach without the wind flipping pages? And that would allow you to look in on the afternoon baseball game every now and then?"[26] That approach also assumes that "software alter egos will learn our interests and guide us in the direction these interests dictate at the level appropriate to our expertise." If there is a level of detail we may not understand, "the hypertext author can make the task easier by hiding from view those things we don't want or need to see."[27]

As can be inferred from the preceding, there is, on the part of our users, the tendency to "attribute infallibility to computer output."[28] A study of the Virginia Tech Library System showed that basic understanding of the VTLS online catalog is "probably no worse than if patrons' perceptions of the card catalog were assessed." Yet there were serious misperceptions about subject searching which "seem to represent the epitome of wishful thinking." This is interesting because the users chose to use the online catalog and seem to have invested much more faith in it.[29] A 1981 study found great user satisfaction with an online catalog despite the lack of subject access and well advertised limitations and incompleteness of holdings.[30] Finally, almost every reference librarian would recognize the inflated expectations many users bring to online database searches. The impression is that computer access to the information they need will solve the problem, no matter how esoteric or complex. For instance, I have never seen a printed citation and abstract mistaken as *the* information source (versus the actual text itself), while I have often seen the online/cd-rom equivalent taken as such. Whether the process utilizes an online catalog, database or cd-rom, information technology delivers *information* simply because of its social context, whether there is a print equivalent or not. That end product has a higher status as well and we find that in our patrons.

In sum, information has been reified by its attendant technology and this in turn has tended to elevate the processes of retrieving information. From the brief review provided, there seems to be a shift away from the book format because of the inherent nature of the capabilities of information technology. There is no question that this will also shift some emphasis away from service to people as well. The example of the online catalog and hypertext book are both steps toward expecting technology to answer questions. Reference service decisions are by definition given over to those machines. I am *not* making the case that we currently are not servicing people and books, but that the context of information, as a reified form, *is* shifting us away from these in subtle ways.

The last area of critical examination of the information broker is the change in the reference librarian itself. If the information broker is to be the wave of the future, then we should assess the change away from the older concept of the reference librarian. James Govan again summarizes it well: "To the degree that libraries become retailing shops, to that degree will librarians cease to be professionals and will become shopkeepers, of necessity. Among the many qualities lost will be . . . a whole host of intangibles that make libraries the civilizing influences they are."[31]

This change seems most clear in descriptions of what a librarian (and the services offered) will be. The model of the corporate database manager was referred to earlier.

> The database manager has certain responsibilities that librarians have been unwilling to assume in the past. . . . The information the database manager provides had better be right. . . . The high priesthood and the mystique that have grown up around computers, data processing and database management software serve the needs of the database manager very well.[32]

A description of the "computer mediated library" drives home the abstractness of future work.

> A reference librarian frequently responds to a reference question without every touching traditional printed materials. An online database search may be conducted for an absent patron and the resulting printout mailed directly to the requestor. The library staff may be removed from the raw material, the product which results from the process, and perhaps even the user of that product.[33]

It has been further suggested that librarians are merely forming the base market demand for the introduction of information services to people directly in their homes.[34]

It seems clear that we are changing not only the form and content of the library, but also the librarian. As early as 1967 it was seen that "the very character of persons integrated in such systems must be compatible with them (and) this means a redefinition of the concept, 'librarian.' "[35] This has come to mean that the changes are bringing "new career paths for librarians who are not necessarily book people, as we once (it now seems almost quaintly) referred to ourselves."[36]

## *LINKS TO LARGER ISSUES*

In identifying ways in which the information broker concept/context might be pulling us away from traditional reference goals, I do not see that librarians alone are making the shift. Rather, these changes are the library and reference manifestations of larger social and economic changes. In this section I would like to link the critique of the information broker to some social analyses in order to better understand, and therefore judge and guide change. It is not within the scope of this paper to provide a full-scale review of these analyses, so I will only briefly review them with special focus on their application to library and reference fields.

The first of these larger issues is the fate of the book itself and the resulting implications. Libraries and reference services are not leading an attack on the book. Rather, they are pulled along in the wake of social and technological change in society. The book and literacy have been in decline for a while now—Bloom's *Closing of the American Mind* and Hirsch's *Cultural Literacy* are only the two most recent looks at the symptom. Television has been cited as the principal villain in the decline. The argument is that our pattern of television watching results in traits like

> difficulty in concentrating and sustaining an extended line of thought in reading and writing . . .; lack of facility in analytic and synthetic reasoning; deficiencies in reasoning back and forth from the concrete to the abstract, the personal to the impersonal, and the literal to the figurative, and in perceiving irony, ambiguity, and multiplicity of points of view.[37]

Neil Postman takes a very similar approach and extends the analysis to the question of whether television fundamentally changes the nature of rationality itself.[38]

I would suggest a theoretical link between what television does to the skill of reading and what information brokerage does to the format of the book. Consider the following:

Television's most successful techniques — short segments, fast action, quick cuts, fades, dissolves — break time into perceptual bits. Reading requires perceptual continuity to track line after line. Television habituates the mind to short takes, not to continuity of thought required by reading.[39]

and

'(Books will be broken down) in fragments suitable for storage in giant computers and for transmission through a variety of audio-visual systems.' No one will want to labor to make a book a coherent whole if everything of that sort is destined to be dismantled into fragments suitable for storage and retrieval.[40]

I contend that the link is not illusory and that libraries and reference services are at perhaps a crucial pressure point in their services to book collections. We could greatly affect approaches to research and knowledge in that "The equipment may not only determine what we will study, it will significantly determine what will be accepted as meaningful data."[41] Further, the context we create for books will have an effect as well. Will we channel use *toward* those new forms to the detriment of the patron? ("It is as though with the invention of food processors we are determined to consume only food capable of being sliced, diced and pulverized."[42]) Our relationship to the book and the social and educational ramifications are important. We should consider the question Derek Bok identifies very seriously.

(There is) the risk of undermining forms of knowledge and understanding that are not quantifiable or reducible to formal processes and rules. As one author puts it, "the issue is not whether the computer can be made to think like a human, but whether humans can and will take on the quantity of digital computers."[43]

The second larger issue has links to the reification and privatization of information. This is the view that technology is *not* a neutral factor. The history of technology as we have come to understand it is underwritten by the assumptions of the "happy technologist": "technology is just a passive tool whose consequences depend on the use to which it is put . . .; there are no values embedded in technology . . .; (it) plays an entirely passive role with respect to issues of power and control . . .; (its purpose) is to satisfy human needs."[44] Those assumptions are false. Technology and technological systems are inherently political and they represent *choices*. For example, we cannot easily refuse to buy a car or refrigerator, whether or not we oppose those technologies, simply because the introduction of them has given rise to social forms (distribution of food and transportation) which need the refrigerator and the car for millions of people to function. Another example is the decline of public transportation. The choice to build the interstate highway system directly led to our great reliance on the car (and car manufacturers) and was most certainly made in a political context.[45] The mere design and construction of a highway is a technical and political decision with social results.[46] We now from the environmental problems posed by automobiles that technology could have dire unintended results.

Lest one think of information technology as an exception to this history, there are strong theoretical links between the computer and earlier, industrial technical innovation.

> One should not seek the origins of the 'Information Society' in the computer chip but in the steam engine. The computer represents only the latest, albeit, crucial, version of the long line of 'control technologies' that have emerged to satisfy an industrial(izing) society's need to control its increasingly fast and vast activities.[47]

A small example of the non-neutrality of the computer in society is the growth of the business of direct mail marketing. The result has been a fine demographic coding of the population which can then be sorted and sold (sound familiar?). But the underlying reasons were the introduction of the information technology which enabled the identification and grouping of people, and then the choice to cut bulk mail rates based on computer sorting of letters.[48] This form of business (good or bad) would not have been possible without the computer, nor the economic choice to lower the bulk (junk) mail rates.

Like earlier manufacturing technology, the computer has abstracted the product it produces and the process by which it is produced. We long ago reached the point where modern production has put a *supply* of "artifacts always . . . ready and available for manipulating, consuming or discarding. . . . The kinds of articles which are mass produced . . . consists of objects with no inherent value apart from human use. Like plastic, their whole form is dependent on human decisions . . ."[49] Information has become the latest form of plastic. It was referred to earlier that we often imbue machines with metaphorical qualities, the "Myth of the Machine" as Lewis Mumford called it. In so doing we turn over social and political direction and the asking of questions to the technology because we consider its triumph inexorable.[50] The result is an identification of those problems prone to technological solution and conforming social values to the imperatives of technological change.[51]

In this incomplete review of the issue, links to reification and privatization of information in the library field are clear. Much of the technical innovation is from outside sources seeking to develop the library market. Our decisions to invest in them have been made in the swirl of Information Society talk. The abstraction of information as a product is in line with the abstraction of work and social relationships brought about by industrial technology. Reification of information has allowed us to attribute social values and ends to information (witness the Information Society binges), and privatization of information is now part of the politicized realm of information policy decisions. As results of information technology, each of these has historical precedent in earlier technologies.

The final link to larger issues sheds light on the changes in the definition of the reference librarian. As a broad explanation I would suggest a link between the hype that the computer has received and librarians' perennial concern over a poor (or lowly) public image. The first of these is the hype that information technology has received. Theodore Roszak has recorded the massive picture of the overselling of the computer to the point where

Ironically, the worst casualty of the megahype may be the computer itself. It is a remarkable invention that deserves our admiration over a wide range of uses. But at the hands of its enthusiasts, this ingenious machine is reduced to a trivial plaything, the carrier of silly, sybaritic values . . . One computer scientist . . . blithely tosses off the remark: "I think there'll be an all-knowing machine someday. That's what we're about."[52]

The hype has been concentrated on schools, a lucrative market of the present which should (as the thinking goes) pave the way for a booming market of the future. As a result, schools have been the target of massive "information" about the need for computers and computer literacy so that students can be competitive and marketable when they look for jobs or colleges. The basis of this reasoning has been heavily criticized as uncritical and not attuned to many (or most) job markets or meaningful social participation. The thrust seems to be the profits to be had from selling the machines and reduced training costs for those who will utilize them.[53] "There is something myopic — and quintessentially American — about this fascination with electronic, glow-in-the-dark technology.[54] "No one wants to be labeled a neo-Luddite, an anti-technologist, a nongrowth person, a methaphobe and computer-anxious one, the kind of person who would have opposed Gutenberg and Copernicus . . ."[55]

This hype has translated easily over to libraries. An example is the Scholar's Workstation Project at Brown University. The general buildup was immense, the university library was to be profoundly altered in the process, and all sorts of fundamental changes were to be expected (especially in the relationship between the library and the computing center). Yet the project has ground down with vastly lowered expectations both in terms of the total number of workstations and their capacities. The project was, by the admission of its originator, a victim of its own hype.[56]

The image and status problems of librarians are semi-legend within the profession. An article by Donald Freeman nicely sums up the historical issue, exploring the low pay and gendered status of the librarians.[57] The current approach has been a frank admission of an image problem with links to information technology seen as the solution. "Computer technology has offered a welcome opportunity to change this stereotype. . . . The librarian's work (is) no longer imprisoned in an obsolete gentility. . . . This new technology has become a symbol of the liberation and invigoration of library science."[58] And: "(There is a) general societal reverence for and fascination with technology. Our use of computers and allied technology will probably increase the likelihood that personnel departments . . . can be led to regard our work in a less stereotyped way . . ."[59]

If there is much doubt that we have either fallen prey to or are participating in the hype, there are plenty of writings which offer examples linked to the library field: "expert systems . . . offer librarians an exciting area in which to carry their profession to a higher level of achievement and recognition. . . . For librarians the information machines open breathtaking possibilities."[60] Put at its simplest, our traditional anxiety about image, combined with the high status of information technology, has let us into some uncritical approaches to new technologies. This in turn is widely acknowledged to be changing the definition of "librarian" in general, and moving the reference librarian toward the more prestigious (and lucrative?) image or information broker. In so doing, we are leaving behind some of the values which have established and anchored reference service.

## CONCLUSION

This paper has been an effort to identify the bases and meanings of traditional reference goals and find in them good aspects of reference librarianship that we may be leaving behind in the shift to information broker. In identifying and critiquing this shift, I examined some evidence and thought already present in the library field and I then provided a framework for them, and then finally linked them to larger social issues. To conclude, I would like to pose some possibilities and questions from the directions of our profession and those areas that influence it.

The first of these is the possibility that, if we do chose to roll our dice with the information broker approach, the result may be a *de-*

*skilling* of the profession. Almost all predictions about information technology and librarianship depict a rise in status and sophistication of work, but there is some evidence that information technology systems ultimately take away professional autonomy. Daniel Dennett has explored the ways in which expert systems can, through a congruence of development and the professional ethics of doctors, deskill one of the most autonomous and prestigious professions. He sees a species of doctor, the "seat of the pants diagnostician," as leading a very challenging, rewarding, exciting but doomed existence.

> A subspecies of doctor will . . . become extinct, succeeded by a new species that will delegate more and more diagnostic responsibility to expert systems, not because of their indolence or stupidity, but simply because they will not be able to defend the claim that they can do as well or better without the system.[61]

Lest one think of this as sheer doom and gloom speculation, this point was driven home almost verbatim in a recent newspaper report on a study of unnecessary medical care.[62] The question becomes, is it realistic for librarians to expect information technology to empower our profession in the long run? There is a long history of technology rendering certain work forms obsolete. The problem is that those qualities and values embedded in that work also become obsolete. I have reservations about helping to develop and create products and markets which may destroy those qualities and values contained within libraries and librarianship.

Secondly, librarianship *is* definitely moving toward the private and entrepreneurial. Whether it is manifested in subscription and use of online databases, the search for additional sources of revenue, user charges or restricted access to research collections, the trend is reasonably clear. This is, I believe, one of the most radical departures from one of our nobler goals: to provide free and open access to books and information to promote informed democracy and the public good. Our libraries and our profession are severing their universal educative role for a partial one: some libraries are open to the public, some services are free, some resources are for the public. Libraries are not profitable in the cost-benefit mode of analysis, and never will be. Their good is not quantifiable and represents as much a faith and public value than a specific service. James Govan asks a question that can be applied to all libraries and their services. "If library service becomes predominantly market driven, what will become of the long-standing commitment of research libraries to the scholarly community . . .? Who then will speak for the public good?"[63] Librarianship, like teaching, law, and medicine is not a private profession. The changes in all those professions have great social importance and they are treated as public issues. Should the effects of our decisions be weighed less?

Finally, I pose the question, do we really *want* to work as information brokers? There is something basic and necessary about what we do, why we do it, what we do it with, and where we do it. Progress has a checkered history, not a glorious one. I would maintain that it would be true progress in our profession only if we harness information technology to serve established goals. Librarianships' notorious/redoubtable conservatism should not be shed so lightly. We work in a context of public values that are important and good (no matter how misunderstood). Nothing should move us from that base.

## REFERENCES

1. Miller, Constance and Rettig, James. "References Obsolescence." *RQ* 25 (Fall 1985): 52-53.

2. Foss, Sam Walter. "Some Cardinal Principles of a Librarian's Work." In *American Library Philosophy: An Anthology*, edited by Barbara McCrimmon. Hamden, Conn.: Shoe String press, 1975: 31.

3. "Mission of a University Undergraduate Library: Model Statement." *College and Research Libraries News* (October 1987): 543.

4. Bostwick, Arthur E. "The Love of Books as a Basis for Librarianship." In McCrimmon: 30.

5 Handlin, Oscar. "Libraries and Learning." *American Scholar* 56 (Spring 1987): 213.

6. MacLeish, Archibald. "The Premise of Meaning." in McCrimmon: 230-31.

7. Dalrymple, Prudence W. "Closing the Gap: The Role of the Librarian in Online Searching." *RQ* 24 (Winter 1984): 177-78.

8. Miller, Constance and Rettig, James: 52-58.

9. DeLoughry, Thomas J. "Once They Asked: How Many Library Books? Now It's: Are Computers Available at 3 a.m.?" *The Chronical of Higher Education* (September 14, 1988): A39.

10. Dougherty, Richard M. and Lougee, Wendy P. quoted in Cart, Michael. "Caveats, Qualms, and Quibbles: A revisionist View of Library Automation." *Library Journal* (February 1, 1987): 40.

11. Examples abound like Oscar Handlin's article and others: "The Future of the Printed Word." *USA Today* (March 1987): 88-90, and Schieber, Paul and Lewis, Page. "Noted Scholar Brooks Stresses Value of 'Literature in a Technological Age' During 1985 Jefferson Lecture in the Humanities." *Research Libraries in OCLC* 17 (Autumn 1985): 5-6.

12. Especially Gray, Carolyn M. "Information Technocracy: Prologue to a Farce or a Tragedy." *Information Technology and Libraries* (March 1987): 3-9.

13. Haar, John M. "The Politics of Information: Libraries and Online Retrieval Systems." *Library Journal* (February 1, 1986): 41.

14. Campbell, Brian. "Information Access and Technology." *LITA Newsletter* 9 (Summer 1986): 11.

15. Campbell, Brian.

16. Govan, James F. "The Creeping Invisible Hand: Entrepreneurial Librarianship." *Library Journal* (January 1988): 35-38.

17. Fayen, Emily Gallup. "Beyond Technology: Rethinking 'Librarian.'" *American Libraries* (April 1986): 240-242.

18. Baldwin, James Mark, ed. *Dictionary of Philosophy and Psychology*. Gloucster, Mass.: Peter Smith, 1960. Vol. II: 439.

19. Roszak, Theodore. *The Cult of Information: The Folklore of Computers and the True Art of Thinking*. New York: Pantheon, 1986: 16.(I will not recount his full argument here which is contained in pp. ix-71.)

20. Roszak, Theodore: ix-x.

21. Peters, John Durham. "The Control of Information." *Critical Review* 1 (Fall 1987): 6-13.

22. Peters, John Durham: 14-15.

23. Weizenbaum, Joseph. "On the Impact of the Computer on Society." In *Libraries in Post-Industrial Society*, edited by Leigh Estabrook. Phoenix: Oryx Press, 1977: 192.

24. Hernon, Peter and McClure, Charles R. "Library Reference Service: An Unrecognized Crisis-A Symposium." *Journal of Academic Librarianship* 13 (May 1987): 69.

25. Rice, James. "Serendipity and Holism: The Beauty of OPACs." *Library Journal* (February 15, 1988): 139-40., Another Example is Sandler, Mark, "Terminal Ailments Need Not Be Fatal: A Speculative Assessment of the Impact of Online Public Catalogs in Academic Settings." *RQ* (Summer 1985): 460-465.

26. DeBuse, Raymond. "So That's a Book . . . Advancing Technology and the Library." *Information Technology and Libraries* 7 (March 1988): 16.

27. DeBuse, Raymond: 15. 14.

28. Sandler, Mark: 462.

150    *The Reference Library User: Problems and Solutions*

29. Steinberg, David and Metz, Paul. "User Response to and Knowledge about an Online Catalog." *College and Research Libraries* 45 (January 1984): 68-70.

30. Moore, Carole Weiss. "User Reactions to Online Catalogs: An Exploratory Study." *College and Research Libraries* 42 (July 1981): 295-302.

31. Govan, James F.: 38.

32. Fayen, Emily Gallup: 241-42.

33. Johnson, Peggy. "Implementing Technological Change." *College and Research Libraries* 49 (January 1988): 41.

34. Haar, John M.: 34.

35. Graziano, Eugene E. "'Machine-Men' and Librarians, An Essay." *College and Research Libraries* 28 (November 1967): 404.

36. Nielson, Brian quoted in Cart, Michael: 41.

37. Lazere, Donald. "Literacy and Mass Media: The Political Implications." *New Literary History* 18 (Winter 1987): 238.

38. Postman, Neil. *Teaching as a Conserving Activity*. New York: Delacorte, 1979.

39. Lazere, Donald: 240.

40. Lacey, Paul A. "Views of a Luddite." *College and Research Libraries* 43 (March 1982): 111.

41. Lacey, Paul A.:114.

42. Bonham, George W. "Computer Mania: Academe's Inadequate Response to the Implications of the new Technology." *The Chronicle of Higher Education* (March 30, 1983): 72.

43. Bok, Derek. "Looking into Education's High-Tech Future." *Harvard Magazine* (May-June 1985): 35.

44. Balabanian, Norman. "Presumed Neutrality of Technology." *Society* 17 (March/April 1980): 10.

45. Balabanian, Norman: 12-13.

46. Mueller, Milton. "Technology out of Control." *Critical Review* 1 (Fall 1987): 27.

47. Peters, John Durham: 6.

48. Samuelson, Robert J. "Computer Communities." *Newsweek* (December 15, 1986): 66.

49. Mitcham, Carl. "What is the Philosophy of Technology?" *International Philosophical Quarterly* 25 (March 1985): 81.

50. See Mitcham, Carl and Weizenbaum, Joseph.

51. An excellent example of this is Noble, Douglas. "Computer Literacy and Ideology." In *The Computer in Education: A Critical Perspective*, edited by Douglas Sloan, New York: Teacher's College press, 1984.

52. Roszak, Theodore: 37.

53. Noble, Douglas. and Roszak, Theodore.

54. Connolly, Paul. "Our Fascination with Electronic Technology is Myopic and Quintessentially American." *The Chronicle of Higher Education* (September 22, 1982): 48.

55. "Introduction: On Raising Critical Questions About the Computer in Education." In Sloan, Douglas: 1.

56. Moran, Barbara B., Surprenant, Thomas T. and Taylor, Merrily E. "The Electronic Campus: The Impact of the Scholar's Work-station Project on the Libraries at Brown." *College and Research Libraries* (January 1987): 5-17. Brown is not alone in matters of technological overstatement. While implementing a new library system and a new multipurpose building at my former university, the President repeatedly asserted that students and faculty would be able to access the holdings of many other libraries through the network in the new building and the new library system, even after he had been informed otherwise.

57. Freeman, Donald J. "Recognition of Merit: Its Effect on Pay Equity." *Library and Administrative Management* 1 (January 1987): 23-30.

58. Boorstin, Daniel quoted in Berry, John. "Bash a Librarian, Save a Book." *Library Journal* (June 1, 1987): 6.

59. Wilkens, Betsy and Kirkpatrick, Liz quoted in "Image: How They're Seeing Us." *American Libraries* 17 (February 1986): 94.

60. Molholt, Pat. "The information Machine: A New Challenge for Librarians." *Library Journal* (October 1, 1986): 47, 49.

61. Dennett, Daniel C. "Information, Technology, and the Virtues of Ignorance." *Daedalus* 115 (Summer 1986):139.

62. Drake, Daniel C. "Medicine's Jagged Edge: Volumes of Unnecessary Care." *Philadelphia Inquirer* (September 19, 1988): 1A, 8A. The quote, from Edward J. Stemmler, Vice president of the University of Pennsylvania Medical Center, is as follows: "The physician no longer has the kind of academic freedom to say 'I'm going to do it my way. . . .' There's a body of knowledge showing that there's a preferred way and he better damn well do it the preferred way."

63. Govan, James F.: 38.